IMAGES
of America

NORTHWEST AIRLINES
THE FIRST EIGHTY YEARS

Geoff Jones

ARCADIA
PUBLISHING

Published by Arcadia Publishing
Charleston, South Carolina

Printed in the United States of America

Library of Congress Catalog Card Number: 2005922112

For all general information contact Arcadia Publishing at:
Telephone 843-853-2070
Fax 843-853-0044
E-mail sales@arcadiapublishing.com
For customer service and orders:
Toll-Free 1-888-313-2665

Visit us on the Internet at www.arcadiapublishing.com

A Northwest Airlines Airbus A320 departs runway 30 right at Minneapolis/St. Paul in the late
1990s. Downtown Minneapolis provides the backdrop.

CONTENTS

ACKNOWLEDGMENTS

The pictorial material in this book has been obtained from many sources, notably the NWA History Centre Inc. located in Bloomington, Minnesota, and from the author's own aviation photo library.

Many individuals, employees, and former employees of Northwest Airlines have assisted in the assembly of material for this book; particularly Doug Killian and his international corporate communications staff at Northwest's Eagan headquarters, prior to September 11, 2001. More recently H.V. "Pete" Patzke, president of the NWA History Centre Inc., has provided a wealth of information. Pete and his ever helpful band of voluntary enthusiasts (particularly Jerry Nielsen and Bill Marchessault) run and are involved with the History Centre, which was first opened in October 2002 as a non-profit corporation. The History Centre is run by volunteers— retired and current employees of NWA, plus several other interested individuals, all of whom are helping to preserve and archive Northwest's rich and colorful history, gleaned from related private collections and donated gifts. The History Centre is not a part of NWA, nor in any way sponsored by NWA. Also in the History Centre are material from other "family" airlines related to Northwest: Republic Airlines, Hughes Air West, Pacific, Empire, and many other antecedent airlines of the current Northwest Airlines. To contact the History Centre, view their web site www.nwahistory.org or call (952) 997-8000, extension 6102.

Other contributors whose photos, material, and advice have formed an important part of this book include: John Underwood (California), Jon Proctor (Idaho), Chuck Stewart (California), Terry Love (Wisconsin), John A. Whittle (Air Britain DC-4 specialist), Tony Carre, Rod Simpson, George Pennick (all in the UK), Françoise Maenhaut (Airbus), Kristen Loughman (Pinnacle Airlines, Inc), and Björn Larsson (www.timetableimages.com).

Several previously published books about Northwest and its predecessor airlines have also provided helpful background information in the compilation of this book and are recommended for anyone wanting a greater insight into the history of Northwest Airlines:

Airlines of the United States since 1914 by R.E.G. Davies (1972, Putnam, London)
Northwest Airlines by Geoff Jones (1998, Plymouth Press/Ian Allan)
Aircraft in NW Airlines History by Capt. David R. Lane
More than Meets the Sky by Stephen E. Mills (1972, Superior Publishing Co., Seattle)
Flight to the Top by Kenneth D. Ruble (1986, Viking Press)
Ceiling Unlimited "The Story of North Central" by Robert Serling (Walsworth Publishing, Marceline, Missouri)
Northwest Orient by Bill Yenne (1986, Bison Books Ltd.)

Geoffrey P. Jones,
Guernsey, Channel Islands, British Isles.
May, 2005

INTRODUCTION

Northwest Airlines is the operating name of NWA Inc., headquartered in Eagan, Minnesota. It is one of the world's top ten largest airlines and the fourth largest U.S. airline. Now often referred to as a "legacy carrier"—a reference to both its history and pedigree—it is also one of the United States' oldest airlines, founded in 1926 and operating its first scheduled air mail service on October 1st of that year. It is the U.S.'s oldest carrier with continuous name identification, although back in 1926 it was founded as Northwest Airways Inc.

With over 40,000 employees worldwide, Northwest currently provides scheduled services to 113 domestic destinations along with 42 international destinations, all accounting for about 1,500 daily flight departures. Its strong links with the Pacific Rim, and particularly "the Orient," began with its pioneering trans-Pacific services. It is now the largest U.S. carrier between Japan and the U.S., with Tokyo one of its major "hub" airports, along with Minneapolis/St. Paul, Detroit, Memphis, and, through its long-standing alliance with Dutch airline KLM, Amsterdam.

Like most large 21st-century airlines and certainly all "legacy carriers," Northwest has expanded through partnerships, alliances, and subsidiaries, which combined embrace services to 900 cities worldwide in 160 countries and on six continents. Northwest's membership in the SkyTeam alliance was confirmed in September 2004. Northwest, along with partner airlines Continental Airlines and KLM Royal Dutch Airlines, joined the prestigious global airline alliance, now partnering Aeromexico, Air France, Alitalia, CSA Czech Airlines, Delta Air Lines, and Korean Air.

Northwest's domestic status, along with its "fortress hubs," is complemented by its subsidiary airlines, operating what are commonly called commuter services and known as Northwest Airlink (also Northwest Jet Airlink). Mesaba Airlines and Pinnacle Airlines (formerly Express Airlines 1) are major subsidiaries to Northwest, providing passenger "feed" from another 100-plus smaller cities and communities into Northwest's three main U.S. mainland hub airports at Minneapolis/St. Paul, Detroit, and Memphis. Northwest Airlines Cargo is another important subsidiary, particularly in the trans-Pacific market, and Northwest also owns a 40 percent stake in Champion Air, a Minnesota-based charter airline operating Boeing 727-200s.

When Northwest Airways was re-incorporated as Northwest Airlines on April 20, 1934, it had pioneered mail and passenger air services going from the Twin Cities across the western United States to as far as Seattle, and to Chicago in the east. It had mastered the difficulties of year-round, reliable operations, particularly in the harsh winter weather of the northwestern states, it had bought and used all-metal monoplanes, the Ford Trimotor and Hamilton Metalplane, and had pioneered seaplane services to Duluth, Minnesota, using two Sikorsky S-38 amphibians.

Much later Northwest Airlines experienced the "ups and downs" of the U.S. air transport industry, but grew strategically after the Airline Deregulation Act became law in October 1978. Its most notable acquisition was that of Republic Airlines in October of 1986. Republic had previously acquired Hughes Air West and its many predecessor airlines, in addition to Southern Airways, and had evolved from North Central Airways and, earlier, Wisconsin Central Airlines.

Northwest Airlines' history is a microcosm of the history of the U.S. air transport industry, a history of people, planes, and places. It is a history of a strategically vital war effort, along with a world-wide outreach. In 2005, Northwest Airlines is one of the most prominent surviving "legacy carriers" in the U.S. As it battles against the severe competition such "legacy carriers" now experience from up-start rivals, it should not forget its heritage and the dedication of the people who made it great. Any business is a "family" of sorts. Airline businesses have fostered these "family ties" through thick and thin over many decades. While Northwest Airlines endeavors to return to profitability on the eve of its 80th anniversary, in 2006, it must cherish its heritage and its loyal employees, past and present, as important foundations from which to stride out towards even greater goals, and celebration of its centennial in 2026. This book celebrates this first 80 years, and congratulates this airline, a hugely important part of U.S. social history.

In July 1997, Northwest celebrated the 50th anniversary of its scheduled services to "the Orient," which was a general term referring to the Asia/Pacific region. DC-4s, similar to the Berlin Airlift Historical Foundation's C-54 (N500EJ) pictured here, painted in a 1940s-period color scheme for the occasion, flew these first pioneering services. The Boeing 747-227B is N635US, representing the type that flew many of Northwest's trans-Pacific services to "the Orient" from 1970 onwards.

One

NORTHWEST AIRWAYS

Northwest Airways' first flight on October 1, 1926 was a close-run thing. It was an air mail service from Minneapolis/St. Paul's Speedway Field to Chicago and return, C.A.M. 9 (Contract Air Mail No. 9). With three pilots on their books, Charlie "Speed" Holman, Dave Behncke, and Chester Jacobson, and two rented open cockpit OX-5 engine bi-planes, a Curtiss Oriole and Thomas Morse Scout, Northwest's opportunity resulted from the failure of Charles "Pop" Dickinson's enterprise to successfully operate C.A.M. 9.

"Pop," a well known Chicago-based seed dealer, started flying his C.A.M. 9 service on June 7, 1926. By August, it was obvious his enterprise wasn't going at all well; crashes, forced landings, and the resignations of his pilots were just some of Dickinson's problems. He gave the statutory 45 days notice that on October 1, 1926 he'd wind up his new business.

This was Colonel Lewis H. Brittin's opportunity. These were pioneering years—Lindbergh had not yet crossed the Atlantic and President Coolidge was in the White House. Brittin had served as a volunteer artilleryman in the Spanish-American War and in the Quartermaster Corps during World War I. It was here he rose to the rank of Lieutenant Colonel, and from that time onwards was known as "the colonel." An orphan, he passed entrance exams for both Yale and Harvard and entered the Lawrence Scientific School at Harvard, but couldn't afford the fees. During his second year, he left and got a job with a construction contractor, pursuing his studies at night. Jobs in Mexico and then the U.S. with General Electric led him to Minneapolis, where he was instrumental in organizing and planning the Northwest Terminal (unrelated to the yet-to-be-formed airline), a latter-day new industrial park with vital railroad infrastructure. Following this success, the St. Paul Association put Colonel Brittin in charge of some of their business development activities. One of these was to attract the Edsel B. Ford Reliability Tour to St. Paul in 1926.

At the time, auto manufacturer Henry Ford was starting to promote aviation as well as automobiles. In 1925, the first "tour," with 20 assorted aircraft, flew from Dearborn, Michigan, to several cities in the Midwest to promote aviation and flying. The 1925 "tour" missed Minneapolis/St. Paul completely. But the second tour, in August 1926, travelled northwest out of Chicago and Milwaukee to St. Paul, before turning south to Des Moines, thanks to Brittin's cultivation of friendship with several Ford associates and Detroit industrialists. As a result of these "friendships," Henry Ford himself agreed with Brittin that an unused government power dam across the Mississippi near St. Paul and Minneapolis should be turned back to power generation. Ford also agreed to the establishment of an automobile assembly plant close to the dam, the first he built outside the Detroit area.

Brittin had quickly gained a huge amount of respect within the Twin Cities' business community. He was excited by "Pop" Dickinson's establishment of the first air mail service from the Twin Cities to Chicago, but dismayed when Dickinson confided in him, around the time of the Ford Air Tour's arrival in St. Paul, that he was going to have to bail out of this new enterprise by October 1 and that the Twin Cities would be without an air mail service once again. These early years of commercial flight in the U.S., the 1920s, were primarily focused in mail service. Aircraft were not sufficiently developed or reliable for the carriage of passengers. This was one of the Ford Air Tour's objectives—to promote air-mindedness and the development of better commercial aircraft types. But air mail was important, spurred by the 1925 Act and availability of suitable biplane designs.

Brittin went into overdrive when he heard the bad news from Dickinson. Could he get the money, a licence, the aircraft, and the pilots to get a new replacement enterprise off the ground by October 1, 1926? He was going to make damned sure he'd do his best, so he set about looking for an "airline" operation he could substitute for Dickinson's. When this proved unsuccessful, he phoned his friends at Ford in Detroit. He quickly persuaded 29 Detroit businessmen that his new air mail venture was viable, and with a stock value of $300,000, Northwest Airways was incorporated on September 1, 1926, as a Michigan corporation.

With one month to go, Brittin was despatched to Washington with his business plan for a $2.75-per-pound bid for the C.A.M. 9 air mail operation. The Post Office Department accepted the bid and Harold H. Emmons was elected the first director and president of Northwest Airways, Inc.; Frank W. Blair was elected director and treasurer; William B. Stout was elected director and secretary; and Brittin became director, vice president, and general manager. Already a member of this quartet, Stout was a respected aircraft designer, one of his all-metal aircraft had participated in the 1925 Ford Reliability Tour, and his "new, enormous," and revolutionary Stout/Ford Trimotor was a star of the 1926 tour.

As far as aircraft were concerned, Brittin approached Detroit-based Eddie Stinson and agreed to buy (it is thought for a figure of $74,000) three of the latest Stinson Detroiter biplanes with enclosed cockpits. However, Stinson couldn't deliver these new aircraft until November 1926, so Brittin hurriedly arranged a short-term lease on two other biplanes from his friend Bill Kidder: a Curtiss Oriole and Thomas Morse Scout. Next, it was pilots he needed, and he recruited three of the best, Dave Behncke, Chester Jacobson, and the already-famous air race and stunt-plane pilot, Charles "Speed" Holman.

On October 1, 1926, Northwest Airways' first flight, carrying air mail only, departed from Speedway Field (now the site of the Minneapolis/St. Paul International Airport) en route to Chicago. A new era and a future U.S. institution had gotten off the ground by the skin of its teeth!

With a strong tie to the Twin Cities, Brittin was keen to bring his new "baby" back home. This was on top of the day-to-day trauma of operating C.A.M. 9 as the fall weather deteriorated towards winter. The cost of sending mail by air between Chicago and Minneapolis/St. Paul was 10¢ per half-ounce and the new airline was carrying an average of only 35 pounds with an income per flight of only $96.25 each way. Occasionally the new airline would carry a single passenger on the route, to complement the mail earnings, but this was a "loss leader," at only $40 per one-way fare.

Several St. Paul businessmen started to take an interest in the new venture, and Brittin persuaded them to buy stock in Northwest Airways. One of these was "Speed" Holman; confident about the future, he invested $2,000, which was half of his annual salary at the time. Northwest finally "came home" in 1929, when it was purchased by a group of Minnesota financiers, headed by Richard C. Lilly, who was then elected airline president.

The first passenger to be flown by Northwest Airways was "press-ganged" by Brittin on July 5, 1927—Byron Webster, a local St. Paul businessman, became the first officially ticketed passenger on the airline, at the start of a 12 and a half-hour "adventure" flying from Speedway Field to Chicago via La Crosse, Madison, and Milwaukee. The flight eventually landed in darkness at 2:30 am on July 6.

Metal, monoplane aircraft would make the young airline, the Stinson Detroiters were supplemented by Hamilton Metalplanes, and then the "revolutionary" 14-seat, Ford 5-AT-C Trimotor in August 1928. In 1931, Northwest started its first service from Minneapolis to Duluth, and, as the city didn't have an airport, acquired two Sikorsky S-38 amphibians which could land in Duluth harbour.

The push westward, the "Northern Transcontinental Line," was always high on the priority list of the airline. Special advisors were brought in, including Amelia Earhart and Charles Lindbergh, as much for publicity as anything. The final link via Spokane to Seattle was achieved by Northwest on December 3, 1933, with Captain Nick Mamer flying a Waco biplane

(Fleet No. 7). Three Lockheed Orions joined the fleet prior to the delivery of the first Lockheed 10 in 1934. Brittin resigned from Northwest following unprecedented U.S. government intervention in transferring all civilian air mail routes to the U.S. Army in February 1934. Shreeve Archer took over, and the new Minnesota-based owners reincorporated the airline as Northwest Airlines Inc. on April 20, 1934.

From 12,097 passengers carried in 1934, Northwest's expansion continued; 37,786 passengers were transported in 1937, and by 1940 the number had risen to 136,797. Lockheed 10As and 10Bs became the backbone of the fleet, followed by the Lockheed 14H "Sky Zephyr," able to fly the prestigious Minneapolis/St. Paul to Chicago route in 1 hour and 45 minutes and the Chicago to Seattle route in 10 hours and 15 minutes. Croil Hunter took over as President in mid-1937. By 1938, three new concrete runways had been built at Wold Chamberlain Field and Northwest had already established a maintenance facility at Holman Field on the banks of the Mississippi. Six Douglas DC-3s were ordered in 1938, each costing $110,000, although some skeptics thought Northwest would have difficulty filling all 21 seats after the 10-passenger Lockheed 10s and 14-passenger Zephyrs. The first DC-3 arrived in Minneapolis/St. Paul in April 1939 (NC21711), although a DC-3 had been leased from American Airlines for crew training in March. In 1939, Virginia "Ginny" Johnson (of Minneapolis) and Dorothy Stump Eaton (of Chicago) became Northwest's first flight attendants.

By June of 1941, passenger revenue exceeded mail revenue for the first time. The airline's fleet consisted of 13 DC-3s, four Lockheed 10As, and, for service use, one surviving Hamilton Metalplane and one Stinson Reliant. The workforce numbered around 880, and at the end 1941, a total of 149,212 passengers had been transported.

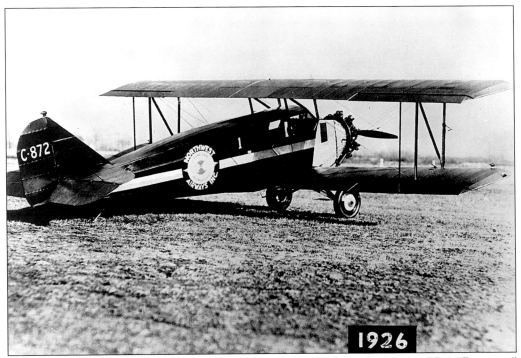

The first new aircraft acquired by Northwest Airways in 1926 was the Stinson SB-1 "Detroiter" C-872. Note the number one on the fuselage side. It was named the "Detroiter" because it was financed by a group of Detroit businessmen. Stinsons were built in Northville, Michigan, at this time; the three for Northwest cost a reported $74,000 to buy. (John Underwood collection.)

This man is believed to be Northwest pilot Walt Bullock alongside Northwest's second Stinson SB-1 "Detroiter" C-873. This aircraft has the number two on the fuselage side. A contemporary mail van is backed up to the Stinson for loading. The SB-1s were the last Stinson biplanes to be built, superseded by the SM-1 Monoplane model.

In front of Northwest's wooden hangar at Speedway Field in Minneapolis (later named Wold Chamberlain Field) is the third of Northwest's new Stinson SB-1 "Detroiter" C-874s with the number three on the fuselage side. The Stinsons were the first enclosed-cabin biplanes used by a commercial airline in the U.S.

Charlie "Speed" Holman, one of Northwest's first three pilots, often flew in a white flying suit. Here he is with a Laird LC-R X-7087 (s/n 167) with several refinements including wheel pants/spats. Compare with the next photo of the same aircraft.

This is another picture of Northwest Airways Laird LC-R X-7087. The inscription *Holman Pilot* can just be seen beneath the cockpit.

This is a Laird LC Mailwing, #2, used by Charles "Pop" Dickinson during his unsuccessful attempt to operate the C.A.M. 9 mail service in 1926, before Northwest took over on October 1, 1926. Underneath the U.S. Air Mail motif are the words, "Chicago-Milwaukee-LaCrosse-Minneapolis-St. Paul." This aircraft was acquired by Northwest in 1927, but may not have been used commercially.

Northwest Airways' stylish logo was adopted in 1927 and advertised "passenger service." A much simpler logo was used initially, as the transport of mail was the purpose of the airline; the first official paying passengers were only flown from July 1927 onwards.

This is the front cover of a September 1928 Northwest Airways timetable. Within the strong link between the airlines—including Transcontinental Air Transport, Inc. (TAT, which later became TWA)—and the railroads, the Pennsylvania Railroad was pioneering.

RAIL PASSENGER SERVICE
via
PENNSYLVANIA RAILROAD
in connection with

AIR PASSENGER SERVICE
Between Chicago and Minneapolis - St. Paul

Effective September 1, 1928

NORTHWEST AIRWAYS, Inc.
and
TRANSCONTINENTAL AIR TRANSPORT, Inc.
in connection with the
PENNSYLVANIA RAILROAD

DAVID N. BELL,
Passenger Traffic Manager,
Philadelphia, Pa.

F. W. CONNER,
Passenger Traffic Manager,
Pittsburgh, Pa.

JAS. P. ANDERSON,
Passenger Traffic Manager,
Chicago, Ill.

This is a classic picture of Northwest Airways' Hamilton H-47 "Metalplane," Fleet No. 24 and NC538E—a revolutionary type first introduced by Northwest in 1928.

Photographed by W.F. Yeager, this Waco JYM "300" is NR42M (s/n 3001) in Northwest Airways colors was employed from 1930 onwards, primarily for "high-speed" mail flights and on "special" company business. It had a faired-in forward cockpit for mailbags and a tapered wing with an M-6 airfoil. It was powered by a 330 horsepower Wright R-975 engine and was flown from the Waco factory in Troy, Ohio, by "Speed" Holman. The fuselage was also 14 inches longer than contemporary Waco ATOs and CTOs. Northwest ordered three JYMs for air mail.

Another Waco biplane in Northwest Airways colors, Waco J-6 NC4576 is now suspended from the roof of the Lindbergh Terminal at Minneapolis/St. Paul International Airport.

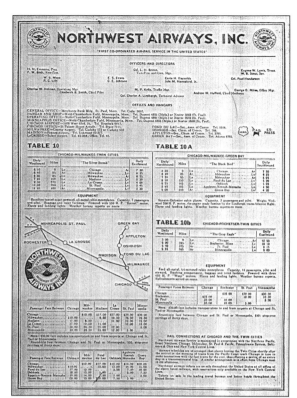

Northwest Airways' timetable and fares poster from 1929 proclaims the "First Co-ordinated Air-Rail Service in the United States."

Signed by Walt Bullock, this picture depicts Bullock arranging for the boarding of passengers into a Northwest Hamilton "Metalplane." Bullock was the nation's youngest licensed pilot; he learned to fly at age 17 in 1916. He became a Northwest career pilot, joining the airline on September 1, 1927, and retiring on March 15, 1961.

Hamilton H-47 "Metalplane," one of nine of these seven-passenger monoplanes flown by Northwest, was powered by a Pratt & Whitney R.1690.A1. This one was Fleet No. 24, as depicted in the previous image. The H-47s served with Northwest for over nine years.

Bob Gilsdorf, Clara Wanvik, Ruth Conrad, and John Vars board a Northwest Airways Hamilton "Metalplane" under the supervision of pilot "Speed" Holman, wearing the airline's new winter attire of a long leather coat with a leather flying helmet and goggles, despite the "Metalplane" having an enclosed cockpit.

Hamilton H-47 "Metalplane" NC7791, Fleet No. 21, a development of the Hamilton H-45, had a 525-horsepower Pratt & Whitney "Hornet" engine and is seen here fitted with wheel skis for typical winter operations on Northwest's scheduled services.

Northwest introduced its first 14-passenger Ford Trimotor in September 1928. It was a revolutionary design by Stout. This fine picture taken by Joe Quigley depicts a Ford 5-AT-C (s/n 5-AT-48), NC8410, Fleet No. 32, in the summer 1932.

Northwest Airways' bustling, new, $100,000 St. Paul facility is pictured on July 1, 1930, as Ford Trimotor NC8419 (Fleet No. 33) prepares to leave for Chicago. Wold Chamberlain airport was retained as an intermediate stop.

A full-page newspaper advertisement from the *St. Paul Daily News* on Sunday, June 15, 1930, depicts Northwest's route system and its Ford Trimotors. Two of the airline's claims in this ad were "Straight as a Homing Pigeon—and on Time" and "Every Possible Comfort for Travelers Aloft."

Ford 5-AT-C Trimotor NC8419, Fleet No. 33, with a "broken fuselage" after an incident at Chicago on August 30, 1933. The caption on the photo says "too much whiskey?" but the cause of the incident was reportedly a nose-over after a wheel failure. This aircraft was later owned by Johnson Flying Services, and was refurbished by Northwest to fly New York to Seattle in 1956 to celebrate the airline's 30th anniversary (see Chapter Three).

Santa Claus, otherwise known as Northwest's chief airplane mechanic, "Big Jim" LaMont, steps from a Northwest Airways Ford Trimotor at Christmastime in 1933. He's holding a model of a Northwest Sikorsky S-38 (see photo below.) Allegedly "Santa's preferred airline," Northwest often flew toys from the North Pole to the needy children of Milwaukee, Chicago, and the Twin Cities during the Depression.

Two Sikorsky S-38 amphibians (NC303N, Fleet No. 40, pictured, and NC199H, Fleet No. 41) were purchased by Northwest in 1931. Northwest wanted to extend its route network northwards from the Twin Cities to Duluth, Minnesota, but Duluth didn't have an airport. Northwest Airways commenced scheduled services with the S-38s on May 30, 1931, landing in Duluth Harbor on Lake Superior.

In 1931, Northwest Airways acquired several second-hand Travelair 6000s while waiting for delivery of its new Lockheed "Orions." NC9933, Fleet No. 46, was built by Walter Beech's Wichita, Kansas company, a development of the smaller Travelair 5000. It provided seating for six, powered by a Pratt & Whitney "Wasp" engine.

Northwest's three Lockheed "Orions" (NC13747, '748 and '749, Fleet Nos. 50, 51, and 52) were first introduced in 1931. Advertised as fast and comfortable, they could cruise at 200 miles per hour and were initially used to link the Twin Cities with Spokane, Washington. The Orions are pictured at Holman Field, St. Paul.

This Lockheed Orion, similar to Northwest's three, is pictured at Grand Central Air Terminal in Glendale, California. When Northwest's Orion passengers (a maximum of six) reached Spokane, they transferred to one of the airline's Hamilton Metalplanes for the flight onward to Seattle and Tacoma.

In 1934, the same year the company's name was changed to Northwest Airlines, the first Lockheed 10-A Electra was introduced. The prototype (NC233Y, Fleet No. 60) was delivered to St. Paul following its first flight on February 23, 1934, with Lockheed test pilot Marshall Headle at the controls. These 10-passenger airliners cost $36,000 each.

Note the "speedboat"-style cockpit windshield with forward raked glazing in Northwest's NC233Y. Northwest purchased 13 Model 10As and a single 10B during 1934 and 1935. The windshield was later modified to a more conventional faired shape.

This mid-1930s Northwest Airlines advertisement characterizes the airline's strong association with the Pacific Northwest and the Rockies.

Former Northwest Vice President and General Manager Croil Hunter was named president and general manager on July 15, 1937, the day this photo was taken.

Northwest Airlines' new Wold Chamberlain maintenance facility in Minneapolis is pictured in this image from 1936 or 1937. The top of the control tower can just be seen in the distance, right, above the hangar roof (also see the next photo).

Lockheed 10A "Electra," NC14262 (c/n 1014), Fleet No. 66, is pictured outside the terminal building and control tower at Wold Chamberlain Field. It was delivered to Northwest on February 28, 1935, but transferred to the United States Army Air Force as a UC-36A on June 14, 1942.

Northwest's Lockheed 10A NC14261, (c/n 1013), Fleet No. 65, does engine runs outside the Lockheed factory in Burbank, California, prior to delivery to the airline on February 9, 1935.

The first Lockheed 14-H Super Electra, the type of aircraft that Northwest called the "Zephyr," X17382, does engine runs outside the Lockheed plant in California. The prototype Zephyr's first flight was on July 29, 1937. Although painted in Northwest Airlines colors, it was never delivered to Northwest. It went to TACA in Central America in December as AN-AAH.

This is another view of Northwest's Lockheed 14-H "Zephyr" X17382 in Burbank, California. The "H" in the designation denotes its Hornet engines. The type certificate for the L-14-H was issued on November 15, 1937, even though Northwest put the type into service on its Twin Cities to Chicago service just prior, in October 1937.

This photo was taken on September 10, 1938, at Northwest Airlines' St. Paul maintenance base, and features a Lockheed 14-H. Note the absence of rudders and ailerons. Years later, Norris Mickleson and Harold Hodgson, who appear in this group, spent many hours identifying everyone who appears in this picture, including Cal Cahoon, who can just be seen in the office window in the rear.

Although passengers were now an important part of Northwest's business, traditional carriage of mail remained pivotal, in addition to early "express deliveries." This 1939 scene includes Northwest Airlines personnel with postal officials and one of the airline's first DC-3s.

Northwest received its first Douglas DC-3, NC21711, in April 1939, although NC21716, pictured, was leased from American Airlines in March 1939, for crew training and service between the Twin Cities and Chicago.

On the ramp at Wold Chamberlain Field, rests Northwest Airlines' Douglas DC-3 NC21715, one of the initial order of ten placed by Croil Hunter at a cost of $125,000 each.

Helen Marzolf Malerich, pictured, was a Northwest Airlines flight attendant between 1944 and 1952, and is seen here with a clipboard, ready to welcome passengers aboard a DC-3 in 1948. Northwest's first flight attendants—or stewardesses, as they were known—arrived in 1939 with the airline's DC-3s. Dorothy Stump and Virginia "Ginny" Johnson were two of the first stewardesses hired.

Northwest used many smaller aircraft for liaison and route-proving flights. NC16870 (c/n 2904) is a Fairchild 24G fitted with a 145-horsepower Warner "Super Scarab" engine. A three-seater, it was first introduced in 1937.

Although pictured in 1976, the Stinson Junior, NC443G, (left) and the Waco biplane, NC1826, are representative of aircraft flown by Northwest Airways in the late 1920s and early 1930s. Both aircraft were owned and restored by Twin Cities-based Boeing 747 captain Daniel F. Neuman (left) and his son Daniel F. Neuman Jr. They were used by Northwest Airlines during 50th anniversary celebrations.

Two

Northwest during World War II

Since its formation, Northwest Airlines had developed a niche market in the U.S. Midwest, together with the development of services to the Pacific Northwest. Its founders and employees had learned the hard way how to run efficient and reliable air services in the bleakest and coldest of climates. The airline had expanded from the 12,097 passengers carried in 1934, and in 1941 carried 149,212 passengers.

Pearl Harbor and the U.S.'s entry into World War II had a rapid effect on every aspect of U.S. life, including the airline business, and Northwest. The army took control of commercial airlines and many of Northwest's flight crews were handed their "call-up" papers. Northwest's schedules—which on the busy Minneapolis/St. Paul to Chicago (Midway airport) route were flown through seven round-trip flights per day—were severely reduced, and some services were cancelled altogether.

Northwest Airlines played three prominent roles in the war effort, although there were many other recorded and un-recorded roles played by the airline and its employees. A bomber modification facility was established at Northwest's Holman Field in St. Paul, with over 5,000 employees engineering and installing special equipment in a variety of strategic war planes. Over 3,000 aircraft were handled there. A similar facility was established at Vandalia, Ohio. The second role Northwest played in the war effort was that the U.S. Army chose Northwest to establish an airborne supply route to Alaska from the rail-head at Edmonton, Alberta, Canada. The route was extended later, by 1,600 miles, to Adak, on the western tip of the Aleutian island chain. The third role played was in the establishment of a new flight training school in Billings, Montana, for the training of Army pilots, particularly those learning to fly the Curtiss C-46 *Commando* cargo aircraft.

The Holman Field modification facility had been established early in World War II and specialized in work on Consolidated B-24 Liberator bombers and North American B-25 Mitchell bombers. It became known as the "Mod." An associated research facility was also established at Wold-Chamberlain Field in Minneapolis where as many as 110 personnel were responsible for investigating de-icing and associated requirements for virtually every aircraft type that entered service with the U.S. Army Air Force. In total the "Mod" dealt with and outfitted 3,286 bombers during World War II. The associated facility at Vandalia, Ohio, known as the Accelerated Service Testing Center, was opened in January, 1943. The first three aircraft of every new model of aircraft manufactured—regardless of manufacturer—were flown to Vandalia, where over 1,000 of Northwest's men and women were responsible for "de-bugging" these aircraft. And unlike the "Mod," Vandalia dealt with fighters, trainers, reconnaissance planes, and even gliders used in the Normandy landings. As well as the research and testing element of the "de-bugging" work, there was considerable administrative work in reporting findings and fixes to the aircraft manufacturer. Speed and secrecy were of the essence.

On February 26, 1942, Northwest signed a contract with the military to establish and then fly the "Flying Boxcar" route to support the war effort in Alaska, which was aimed at discouraging any possible hostile insurgency onto U.S. territory in Alaska by the Japanese. This wasn't as straightforward as it may have seemed. Northwest not only had to fly the route, but first had to establish the infrastructure. It was 2,000 miles from Edmonton, Canada, to Anchorage, Alaska, through some of North America's most hostile territory. With the later addition of the route along the Aleutian Islands, Northwest's Flying Boxcar route totalled 3,986 miles from Minneapolis/St. Paul. Many of the photos taken at this time, showing the guts and determination of the Northwest people on this assignment, were taken by mechanic "Red" Kennedy. He is now 80 years old, and after the war became a Northwest flight engineer and then a pilot. Northwest had to establish airfields—or landing grounds—along the line of the Alaska Highway through the Yukon, notably at Fort St. John, Watson Lake, and White Horse. In the Aleutians, a post at Sheyma Island was established, later to become an important staging post on the airline's commercial services to "the Orient." (See Chapter 3, page 44.)

As well as servicing the U.S. military in their defensive role in Alaska, the route and the airfields along it were important staging posts for U.S.-built aircraft being ferried to Europe "the wrong way round." One of Red Kennedy's photographs from the time depicts Lockheed P-38 Lightnings at Watson Lake amidst the more normal Beechcraft C-45s and Douglas C-47s that were ferrying troops and equipment to and from Alaska. Another veteran of the time, John Peterson—now an ardent supporter of the Northwest History Centre and a Northwest mechanic from 1942 until 1982—remembers the trauma of crews overnighting at some of these airfields in winter. "When a plane arrived we had to drain all the oil from the engines and put it in drums in our heated mess huts. These were quite warm and prevented the oil from freezing. Then the following morning we had to re-fill the engines with the heated oil as quickly as possible and fire 'em up before the oil cooled too much." It was cold and thankless work, but hundreds of Northwest men like John helped to keep the Flying Boxcar route operational and in their own way contributed significantly to the War effort.

Northwest continued to operate commercial services within the U.S. during the war, notably its traditional Minneapolis/St. Paul to Chicago route. While pre-war load factors hadn't been tremendous (around 65%), the pressure of the nation-wide war effort caused the airline's load factor to leap to 85%. Northwest didn't ignore the inevitable return to peace after the war, either. As early as 1943, the airline sent applications to the Civil Aeronautics Board (CAB) to operate on 13 different routes. Routes to New York and Alaska were amongst these, as well as a request to serve Asia. In 1944, another CAB application from Northwest requested authority to serve Honolulu.

On June 1, 1945, Northwest operated its first post-war transcontinental flight using a DC-3 between Seattle and New York for servicemen returning home. But as airlines such as TWA and PanAm were awarded new international routes across the Atlantic, it was the CAB's recommendation that Northwest be certified on a route from New York and Chicago to Asia by way of Minneapolis/St. Paul, Edmonton (Canada), and Anchorage (Alaska). The CAB also approved a Seattle route to Asia via Alaska for Northwest, and on August 1, 1946, President Truman signed the certificate authorizing Northwest to fly these routes.

The route to "the Orient" would be flown with all the experience that Northwest had gained during its war-effort on the Flying Boxcar route and had the newspaper headline writers in over-drive with slogans such as "Northwest Passage By Air" and "Minneapolis Now Sitting On Top Of The World." Northwest made plans to fly the Great Circle route to Asia commercially, and in preparation, on September 1, 1946, operated its first "outside" coastal route from Seattle to Anchorage. On January 2, 1947, Northwest flew the first service on the "inside" overland route from Minneapolis/St. Paul via Edmonton (Canada) to Anchorage.

The survey flights resulted in triumph on July 15, 1947, when Northwest Airlines inaugurated flights from the U.S. to "the Orient": Tokyo, Seoul, Shanghai, and Manila. Flying three times a week, Northwest used its new Douglas DC-4s—under the leadership of Don King, who was appointed the airline's vice president of the "Orient" region. Establishment of landing rights in China, Korea, and the Philippines was one of King's achievements. The establishment of the airport at remote and windswept Shemya Island, at the end of the Aleutian chain, was another—fifty-five Northwest staff members were based here for a year at a time! In 1947, Northwest carried 663,352 revenue passengers. In another twist, Howard Hughes (see Chapter Six), who owned TWA (Trans World Airways), tried to forge a link with Northwest Orient as a way of overcoming the Civil Aeronautics Board's (CAB) stubborn refusal to grant TWA rights to fly the Pacific with his fleet of Lockheed Constellations, part of his aspirations for a round-the-world route for TWA.

The Northwest DC-4 fleet would eventually number 18; 15 of them converted ex-military C-54s, the first of which was delivered to Northwest in March 1946. These complemented the 23 DC-3s that Northwest had in its fleet by 1946. With foresight and courage, in March 1946, Northwest also ordered 10 of Boeing's new "double-deck" Stratocruisers (the model 377-10-30) at a cost of 15 million dollars, primarily for its "Orient" services, able to seat 69 first-class passengers on its upper deck, as well as 14 below. They were distinctive from other "Strats," with square windows on both decks. For short haul work, Northwest placed an order for 10 (increased to 25, and then 40 later) of the un-pressurized Martin 2-0-2s, introducing them in November 1947, wearing the airline's new livery, notably the solid red tail, for the first time—a new compass logo was also adopted. In 1949, the coast-to-coast airfare was reduced to $97 and one newspaper reported that Northwest's load factor on the route was 91%.

The first two Stratocruisers delivered to Northwest were N74602, on June 22, 1949, and N74601, on July 29, 1949, nearly a year behind schedule. The N74602, named *Stratocruiser Minneapolis St Paul*, flew its first revenue service for the airline on August 1 between Minneapolis/St. Paul and Chicago.

Despite a profitable year in 1949, business in the airline world would be difficult. On June 25, 1950, the Korean War broke out when communist North Korean forces invaded South Korea. Northwest was to ground its Martin 2-0-2 fleet after a series of four accidents involving the type in less than a year—the order for 40 aircraft had been reduced to 25 by this time. Northwest's President Croil Hunter was set for a tumultuous ride.

Beech C-45 and Douglas C-47 were photographed by "Red" Kennedy, probably at Watson Lake, Canada, on the Alaska Highway supply line to Fairbanks, Alaska, and beyond. Kennedy was stationed here with Northwest Airlines as part of their vital war effort from 1942 onwards.

The Curtiss C-46 "Commando," or "Flying Boxcar," is seen being loaded with supplies for U.S. Alaskan-based troops in 1943. The logo behind the U.S. military star is "The Air Transport Command—U.S. Army Air Forces." Northwest's "Flying Boxcar" air supply route extended 3,986 miles, from the Twin Cities to Fairbanks or Anchorage, Alaska, and out to the tip of the Aleutian Islands.

In a photo taken by Ray Wiehe, this Northwest Lockheed 10 crew aboard NC14900, Fleet No.67, have delivered urgent wintertime medical supplies to Burwash Landing in the Canadian Yukon on March 23, 1942. The dog sled team took over for the final sector of the delivery.

This "Red" Kennedy picture was taken at Watson Lake in the Yukon in 1942. Kennedy was then an apprentice mechanic serving under Phil Beaudoin. Northwest started by flying C-47s (military DC-3s) on the supply route to Alaska, but C-45s were also common, as can be seen from this picture. Northwest serviced the military ATC pilots, and the numbers and variety of aircraft grew rapidly to include A-20s, B-26s, P-40s, P-38s (one pictured), and P-39s. They also took care of smaller aircraft operated by Bob Reeves who was flying highway surveyors from Watson to Fort Nelson.

Another aircraft type used by Northwest Airlines both during and after the war on survey and training flights was the Cessna T-50, variously known as the "Bobcat," "Bamboo Bomber," "Rhapsody in Wood," and many less complimentary names. NC50197 is pictured during maintenance, probably at Wold Chamberlain.

Northwest's war-time personnel, many of them women, work on a Consolidated B-24 Liberator bomber at the "Mod," St. Paul's Holman Field. The "Mod" dealt with 3,286 bombers during World War II.

A Consolidated B-24 Liberator gets airborne from runway 13 at the "Mod." Wartime downtown "skyscrapers" of the burgeoning Twin Cities can be seen beyond and to the left.

Holman Field, on the banks of the Mississippi River, is pictured as it looked in 2001, home of Northwest's "Mod" center during World War II. Holman Field was finally abandoned by Northwest in 1960, with the move of all operations and maintenance to the new Minneapolis/ St. Paul International airport at Wold Chamberlain Field.

Post-war, Northwest Airlines got back into "proper" commercial operations with a fleet that included Douglas DC-3s, but beginning March 1946, utilized new DC-4s (modified military transport C-54s). NC6421 is pictured on the ramp in Northwest's early post-War colors.

(*right*) This bevy of beauties "high-tails it" on the tail of a newly delivered Northwest DC-4 in the summer of 1946. As post-war commercial flying accelerated, many new staff were required by the airline, including stewardesses. Rosie Stien organized the training these new recruits needed: a three-month course at Zell McConnel's School in Minneapolis.

(*below*) Northwest first flew a 10-hour DC-3 survey flight from Seattle to Elmendorf Field, Alaska, in 1946, in anticipation of commencement of scheduled commercial services to Alaska. In July, the Key to the City of Anchorage was presented to Croil Hunter (second from right, in hat). This was the official party who had flown on DC-4 NC6404 on the "outside route" from Seattle. Northwest expected to start "inside route" services within two months of this inaugural. Schedules to Alaska commenced on September 1.

Also in 1946, Northwest flew two route survey flights to "the Orient" in one of the airline's DC-4s. Northwest was anxious to obtain rights from the governments of China, the Philippines, and Korea, as well as from the occupying army in Tokyo, Japan, under General Douglas MacArthur, to fly service from the U.S.

Northwest commenced a three-times-a-week schedule to "the Orient" on July 15, 1947, even though the U.S. government didn't approve the opening of Japan for tourism for at least a year. NC95413, a DC-4, is pictured taking off from Anchorage en route to "the Orient" later in 1947.

Accidents do happen, and on January 6, 1947, at Chicago's Midway airport, Northwest's DC-4, NC95412 (c/n 18330 and ex 43-17130), hit a concrete marker on its approach to runway 22R. The undercarriage then collapsed, and the DC-4 slewed around and was soon destroyed by fire. Fortunately, all 4 crew members and 37 passengers, under the captaincy of Jack Gault, escaped with no fatalities.

Croil Hunter (Northwest's president) announced a $10 million order for 40 Martin 3-0-3s (later re-designated 2-0-2s) in June 1946. The first was introduced in November 1947, also heralding a "new look" livery for Northwest, the solid red tail. N93051 is pictured flying over Washington D.C.

Described as the "World's Most Modern 2-Engine Airliner," the Martin 2-0-2 started to replace the airline's DC-3s in Northwest service. This postcard depiction was distributed to passengers on Northwest's Martin 2-0-2 flights as a memento, asking passengers to "address, stamp, and return to stewardess who will mail for you."

Resplendent in Northwest's new "red tail" livery, Douglas DC-4 N95413 strikes a classic pose. A new compass symbol was also adopted in 1947–1948 as a part of the revamping, and in 1949, the name Northwest Orient Airlines was first coined.

Northwest DC-4 N95419 is pictured as it arrives from Anchorage, Alaska, at Haneda International, Tokyo, Japan, in 1949. U.S. military "hardware" in the form of Boeing B-17s and C-54s can be seen behind. The plane was photographed in 1949 by Jerry Koerner, the radio operator on the first Northwest flight to "the Orient," in 1947.

Three

AIR SERVICES TO THE ORIENT AND THE 1950s

At the beginning of the decade, Northwest changed its name to Northwest Orient Airlines, although officially still Northwest Airlines Inc. A small italicized "Orient" had already started to appear on some Stratocruiser aircraft between the larger "Northwest" and "Airlines." This change reflected the importance associated with its services to Asia. With the Korean War raging, Northwest was again to feature prominently in a war effort, primarily airlifting troops and equipment from the U.S. to support U.S. troops in South Korea, but also in the operation of seven DC-4s flown by Northwest pilots on the "Korean Airlift" contract within Southeast Asia—this continued into the mid-1950s and carried well over 100,000 military personnel. Northwest also helped with the establishment of Japan's first post-war domestic airline, the fore-runner of All Nippon Airlines.

On September 4, 1952, Northwest's founder, Colonel Brittin, died at the age of 75. Harold R. Harris took over the presidency of the airline on January 1, 1953, but was replaced in October 1954 by Donald W. Nyrop, who at 42 became the youngest president of a major U.S. airline.

The 1954 route system stretched from New York in the east to Hawaii (served from both Portland and Seattle) and Asia, with seven destinations now served: Tokyo (a small hub already), Seoul and Pusan (S. Korea), Okinawa, Taipei (Formosa/Taiwan), Hong Kong, and Manila (the Philippines). The remote airport at Shemya Island was also closed by Northwest in July 1954 as the airline switched its "Orient'" operations to Cold Bay.

From a fleet perspective, the Stratocruisers flew the bulk of the services to Asia from 1952 onwards, some with sleeper compartments and with a lower deck lounge. On their domestic routes, New York to Milwaukee and Minneapolis/St. Paul, some "Strats" featured an on-board organist who provided entertainment. This arrangement was instigated by Minneapolis-based Northwest Organ Co. (at 6436 Penn Avenue South), who sold Lowrey Organs. The feature was billed as "Music in the Sky While You Dine" and played by the well-known organist C.R. "Swanney" Swanson. New airliner developments were taking place at both Lockheed and Douglas. Northwest ordered six L-1049G Super Constellations for its "Hawaiian Express" services and for the long range services to Asia, freeing up the "Strats" for further development of U.S. trans-continental services. Two Super Constellations were actually diverted for delivery to Qantas. N5174V flew the first Northwest Super Constellation service on February 15, 1955, from Seattle to Anchorage.

Northwest was still operating from Holman Field, close to downtown St. Paul and on the flood plain of the Mississippi. A major inundation of the airport in April 1952 was the final straw in a difficult time for the airline following the trouble with its Martinliners. A move to Wold Chamberlain Field, close to the old Speedway Field and now the site of Minneapolis/St. Paul International Airport was a logical step. It wasn't until 1958 that contracts were let for a new Northwest headquarters and overhaul and operations facility, part of an $18 million investment.

For Northwest's 30th anniversary in October 1956, the airline chartered a Ford 5-AT-58 Trimotor (N8419) from Johnson Flying Services of Missoula, Montana, to re-create the early years, after it had been refurbished by the airline's maintenance staff at St. Paul. Flown by two of Northwest's veteran captains, Deke DeLong and Joe Kimm, the aircraft travelled across the U.S. from city to city wearing colors similar to Northwest Airways. There were now 5,500 employees working for Northwest worldwide.

Northwest wanted to expand its route system to less traditional parts of the U.S. The winter cold of its Minnesota home had a ready market for vacationers wanting to travel to Florida's winter sunshine. Several attempts were made before the CAB approved a Chicago to Miami route for Northwest in 1958, and also the same route but via Atlanta and/or Tampa. Authority to fly services to Florida from both Minneaplois/St. Paul and Milwaukee soon followed. Northwest was entering a fiercely competitive market—Eastern and Delta were already strong in the Chicago to Miami market. However, on December 6 of that year, Northwest inaugurated its first north to south service when a "Strat" left Minneapolis/St. Paul bound for Miami.

Other aircraft orders during the 1950s were for the new pressurized Douglas DC-6B (entering service in 1956, with the fleet growing to 20 aircraft), then 14 of the larger Douglas DC-7C. The airline's last Douglas DC-3 (N39544) was retired from service on September 27, 1958, when it made its last commercial landing for Northwest at Seattle-Tacoma—she was sold for $25,000. The imminent arrival of the new jets and the competition from other, newer prop-liners such as the DC-7, spelled the death knell for Northwest's "Strats," and on September 15, 1960, the last one was retired. This wasn't before the most significant event in the whole of Northwest's fleet history in 1958, Donald Nyrop's $67 million spending spree on new aircraft, notably the $28.9 million order for five Douglas DC-8 pure jets, complemented by a $24 million order with Lockheed for 10 of their new L.188 Electra. A huge $14 million was also spent on spares for these new aircraft.

The end was in sight, though, for the "Strats" and some of the DC-7Cs, with costs of $10.231 million being realized from trade-ins of these aircraft. The first Electras started to arrive in July/August 1959, immediately becoming popular with Northwest's clientele. A further eight were ordered at an additional cost of $22.668 million, all helping contribute to one of Northwest's best years so far, with a reported $5.7 million profit.

Northwest took delivery of its first Boeing 377 Stratocruiser—or "Strat" for short—on June 22, 1949. The first two of these double-deck, 75 to 100 passenger airliners were placed in service on the Twin Cities to Chicago route in late July 1949.

Pictured at Elmendorf Air Force Base, Alaska, in April 1952, Northwest's Boeing Stratocruiser *Washington* flies the inaugural Seattle to Tokyo Stratocruiser service.

A 1950s Northwest Airlines baggage sticker depicts a red-tail "Strat."

Honolulu, Hawaii, was also a regular destination for Northwest Airlines Stratocruisers. N74608, Fleet No.708, delivered on October 21, 1949, is seen here in front of the control tower at Honolulu after arrival from Seattle/Tacoma. Note the Polynesian word "aloha" or "welcome," printed diagonally on the front of the tower. This aircraft, named *Stratocruiser Tokyo*, ended its flying days when it ditched in Puget Sound on April 2, 1956.

The tail of Stratocruiser N74604 is pictured in July 1957, when it was flown to James Town, North Dakota, for the local "Air Fair." Note the style of the Northwest *Orient* Airlines on the red tail and the company compass logo current at the time. This aircraft was first delivered to Northwest on August 11, 1949.

Some of the beautiful models of Northwest Orient aircraft are now displayed in the Northwest History Centre in Bloomington, Minnesota. The Lockheed Electra on the right is complemented by the Boeing Stratocruiser on the left, as depicted in the next picture.

Former Northwest Airlines Captain Brooks Johnston is pictured in 1988 or 1989 at a RNPA (Retired Northwest Pilots Association) convention at Las Vegas with a large travel agent's model of one of the airline's Boeing Stratocruisers, restored by Ed Matthews Jr. and donated to the airline by Harry McKee Jr. (see above photo).

A Japanese beauty, wearing traditional Japanese costume, pours champagne over the fuselage of Stratocruiser *City of Tokyo* N74608 on its inaugural flight to Tokyo in 1952.

"Music in the Sky While You Dine" was the attraction aboard Northwest's Stratocruiser 709 in 1959 while flying between New York and the Twin Cities. In conjunction with Lowrey Organs and the Northwest Organ Co. of Minneapolis, organist C.R. "Swanee" Swanson serenaded the passengers. With the "Strat's" 28-volt DC electrical system, the current had to be fed through an inverter to turn it into the 115-volt, 60-cycle AC current used by the organ.

A Northwest Airlines postcard from the early post-war period depicts the luxury Boeing Stratocruiser passengers could expect to enjoy when the "new 80-passenger, pressurized airliner would fly you in comfort high above the clouds." Unfortunately, although the card anticipated being ready for service in early 1947, the service didn't materialize until mid-1949.

Shemya Island at the western tip of the Aleutian Islands archipelago (1,461 miles from Anchorage) was operated by Northwest as a staging post on its great circle route to "the Orient." Northwest was first involved there during World War II, helping to fly 14,000 troops to this inhospitable and rocky U.S. outpost. From 1947 it was nick-named "schmoo" by many Northwest volunteers who were stationed there, 55 at a time for a year at a time, to fuel and service the DC-4s routing from the U.S. to Asia via Anchorage and then on to Tokyo. Bob Johnson and Jim Suaimura are pictured here at the "schmoo" in April 1952. It was de-activated in July 1954.

In February 1955, a Mrs. Takahashi prepares to board Northwest Airlines Boeing Stratocruiser Flight No. 821 at Seattle-Tacoma. Note the carry-on bag displaying the Northwest logo, often provided as a complimentary gift, an essential part of 1950s luggage on most of the world's major airlines at the time.

In 1951, Northwest celebrated its 25th anniversary and 25 years of air mail carriage, with aircraft ancient and modern. Boeing Stratocruiser *New York* (N74604) is posed here with a restored Waco biplane (N3752H), representative of the first aircraft flown by the airline in 1926.

The silver anniversary class of newly graduated Northwest Airlines stewardesses pose on the boarding stairs of a Northwest Douglas DC-4 in September 1951.

For Northwest's 30th anniversary in October 1956, a refurbished Ford Trimotor was flown from Idelwilde airport (New York) to Seattle-Tacoma. The Trimotor was N8419, a Model 5-AT-58 chartered from Johnson Flying Services of Missoula, Montana, and a former Northwest Airways aircraft, originally delivered new to the airline in 1929 and disposed of in 1935. Here Bob Johnson points out features of the aircraft to two of Northwest's veteran pilots, "Deke" DeLong and Joe Kimm. (See photograph on page 19.)

After 20 stops, Northwest's nationwide 30th anniversary Trimotor flight arrives in a wet Seattle-Tacoma. Captain Leon S. "Deke" DeLong is greeted by his wife, Bertie, and Mrs. Art Peterson, wife of Northwest's western region operations manager.

Northwest Airlines traditionally linked the Twin Cities with Chicago. This mid-1950s picture of Chicago's Midway airport features a variety of airlines and types when Midway was the world's busiest airport. Northwest Douglas DC-3 N12935 is accompanied on the ramp by a Wisconsin Central DC-3 (see Chapter Five).

Minneapolis' Wold Chamberlain Field is pictured in the mid-1950s with the 1930s brick terminal and control tower visible. As well as the two Northwest DC-3s and a DC-4, on the left is a Capital Airlines DC-4. (Capital became part of United Airlines.)

Despite flooding from the Mississippi and a restriction on room for any expansion, Northwest maintained its maintenance facility at St. Paul's Holman Field into the late 1950s. This "Red" Kennedy picture shows a Northwest Martin 2-0-2 and Douglas DC-4 (left), N95425, on heavy maintenance at St. Paul.

The final "red tail" livery worn by Northwest's DC-3 fleet, N79056 (c/n 20195) is pictured at Minneapolis in 1957. Northwest's last DC-3 service was on September 27, 1958.

Northwest's first Douglas DC-6B was leased in September 1953. Eventually 25 pressurized DC-6Bs were operated by the airline, many of them on the routes from Seattle-Tacoma and Portland to Honolulu. This Northwest DC-6B is pictured over Waikiki, Honolulu.

Originally six Lockheed 1049G Super Constellations were ordered by Northwest in 1953, the first to be delivered in the spring 1955. With the airline's presidency being taken over by Donald Nyrop, the Constellations didn't feature prominently in his planning, so two were immediately sold. This pre-delivery picture of N8201 is taken over the greater Los Angeles conurbation.

Sub-titled "Casing the Connie," this picture of N5175V was taken at Billings, Montana, on the occasion of the Billings Air Fair held and October 1 and 2, 1955. A reported crowd of 5,000 attended the air fair, most of whom waited for hours for the opportunity to file through the cabin of Northwest's "star attraction."

Douglas DC-4 N350E, Fleet No.433 (c/n 27233), is pictured in Minneapolis c. 1958, shortly before its retirement from Northwest service.

In 1956, Northwest ordered eight long-range, pressurized, 95-passenger Douglas DC-7Cs primarily for service on the great circle route to Asia. A slightly revised color scheme was adopted when the first DC-7C was delivered in 1957—the "DC-7C" was prominent on the tail. The type was part of Donald Nyrop's move to update Northwest's equipment. A total of 17 DC-7Cs eventually flew with Northwest.

A color advertisement from 1957 heralded the proposed delivery of 24 new Douglas DC-7Cs to Northwest *Orient* Airlines. The growing stature of the airline is emphasized, now with 18,000 route miles and a route structure stretching from New York to Japan.

Coronation Coach Service described as "the most gracious experience in the history of flight."

A color postcard image of a Northwest Orient Airlines "Imperial Service" DC-7C (N284) which was "radar equipped and pressurized for your comfort" and offered both Imperial Service and Coronation Coach Service described as "the most gracious experience in the history of flight."

Lockheed Electra, Northwest's first jet-prop airliner, Fleet No.121, is pictured during crew training at Wold Chamberlain Field shortly after delivery to Northwest on July 25, 1959. With the Electra, Northwest also added the "imperial eagle" logo to the tail, signifying the Imperial Service in the cabin that the airline's all-jet fleet would herald. This aircraft tragically crashed in Indiana on March 17, 1960, killing all on board.

With the advent of jet-prop power, Northwest's mechanics had to be re-trained to work on the 3,750-horsepower Allison turbo-prop engines that powered the Electras. This group of engineers worked under the supervision of the Allison Division of GMC between May 11 and May 26, 1959.

Four

NORTHWEST ORIENT FROM 1960 TO 1986

Northwest entered the jet age on July 8, 1960, when the first DC-8-scheduled service to "the Orient" was launched. The DC-8s were able to carry 120 passengers (42 first and 78 coach) and reduced the New York to Tokyo elapsed time by six and one-half hours over their nearest competitor. The year 1960 also saw the last Northwest airliner overhauled at Holman Field, as the airline's move to Wold Chamberlain was completed and the cities of St. Paul and Minneapolis adopted the airport as the Twin Cities airport. The airport's new $10 million "jet-age" terminal was opened in January 1962.

The next jet airliner to join the Northwest fleet in July 1961 was the 111-passenger Boeing 720B; 17 ordered and put into service on their "flagship" route of Minneapolis/St. Paul-Chicago-New York and in December 1962 on the New York-Honolulu route (via Chicago-Seattle-Portland). Incredible growth and increasing profitability were the key words for Northwest in the 1960s, but in 1968, Northwest was still only the U.S.'s seventh largest airline. After the 720s, the first five new Boeing 707-320s were ordered in 1962 for intercontinental services; by 1964 the investment in new fan jet airliners was accelerating, when that same year their first three from an order for 19 new Boeing 727 tri-jets entered service. Northwest's presence and influence in Asia was also boosted by the 1964 Olympic Games in Tokyo and the introduction later that decade by a new Clarence K.M. Lee designed color scheme with prominent "Northwest Orient" titles on the sides of all its fleet, together with a new logo—the red tail, first introduced in the late 1940s, was retained.

By 1966, Northwest Orient Airlines had an all-jet fleet of 61 aircraft and had placed an order, for 1970 delivery, of ten of Boeing's new "jumbo jets," the Boeing 747-100. On June 22, 1970, Northwest's inaugural "jumbo" service was flown between the Twin Cities and New York with President Donald Nyrop and Vice President of Maintenance and Engineering Frank Judd on board. Soon afterward, Northwest became the first airline to offer 747 services across the Pacific from its four major gateways of Seattle, San Francisco, Los Angeles, and Honolulu—five longer-range 747-200s (with a 6,740 mile, non-stop range) were added for these services in 1971.

When a proposed 1969 merger between Northwest and Northeast Airlines failed at the last moment, Delta Air Lines being the successful Northeast suitor. A merger between Northwest and National also came close, but failed, in 1970. And while Northwest had nearly all Boeings in its fleet, Donald Nyrop surprised everyone by placing an order for the Douglas DC-10 "wide-body" tri-jet. However, it wasn't a standard DC-10-30, but a special for Northwest, fitted with the Pratt & Whitney JT9D engine for commonality with its 747 fleet, but also giving Northwest's DC-10s an extra 1,200 mile range over standard models. The first DC-10-40s arrived in late 1972, part of the 22-aircraft order. Northwest's faith in the DC-10-40 was proved when it made a non-stop, 7,677-mile flight between Los Angeles and Hong Kong with Federal Aviation Administration (FAA) officials on board. The flight time was 14 hours and 44 minutes.

Northwest aircraft returned to Peking (now Bejing) at the end 1973, the first time since their pioneering flights, that were terminated in 1949. On the airline's 50th birthday in 1976,

Donald Nyrop resigned and the presidency was taken over by Joe Lapensky. The airline turned a $43.2 million profit that year and had a fleet of 113 aircraft.

Following the Airline Deregulation Act on 1978, competition in the U.S. domestic market became even more fierce. Jet fuel prices doubled in 1979, but despite this Northwest commenced a whole range of new domestic schedules. It also made its first all-cargo flights to Europe following the formation of Northwest Cargo in 1975 (see Chapter 8). Boston and New York cargo service to Glasgow (Scotland) commenced on February 9, 1979, followed on March 31 by the first Northwest trans-Atlantic passenger service from the Twin Cities via Detroit and New York to Copenhagen (Denmark) and Stockholm (Sweden). Passenger service to Glasgow followed on April 28, and then on June 2, 1980, the first Twin Cities to London (Gatwick) schedule, flown by 747-200s. Northwest has flown trans-Atlantic from the Twin Cities to London continually ever since. A new Northwest Boston to London (and onwards to Hamburg, Germany) schedule commenced on April 26, 1981, after a hard-fought battle for these rights against several airlines and several cities seeking new "U.S. gateway" rights.

In 1958, work was underway on Northwest's move to Wold Chamberlain Field, part of an $18 million investment. The airport authority also undertook to build a new $10 million terminal. This was opened on January 13, 1962, amidst much ceremony. This building is still the core of the Lindbergh Terminal at MSP (Minneapolis/St. Paul International) in 2005.

After the jet-prop Electra came the pure jets. Northwest's first was the Douglas DC-8C with a 585-mile-per-hour cruise speed and accommodation for up to 139 passengers. The first was put into service on the trans-Pacific route from Seattle-Tacoma to Tokyo in October 1960. The aircraft N801US, pictured, was one of two DC-8s delivered to Northwest in an earlier color scheme, with blue cheat line above the windows and the name "Northwest" written within it. Compare with the N804US in next the picture.

A pilot's dispute regarding a third pilot delayed regular service entry for Northwest's DC-8s, followed by a flight engineers dispute in October 1960. N804US (c/n 45605) was delivered on September 22, 1960. Note the revised color scheme, compared to the previous photo. This aircraft has a blue cheat line along the window line and "Northwest" written in the white above it.

In this July 8, 1960 image, the Douglas DC-8C N802US arrives amidst considerable ceremony. The event marked Northwest's first trans-Pacific jet service, knocking six and one-half hours of the elapsed flight time between New York and Tokyo compared to its nearest competitors.

Donald Nyrop's spending spree on new jets included 17 of the Boeing 720Bs. The first was delivered in July 1961. In December 1962, the type was introduced on the New York to Honolulu route, flown via Chicago, Seattle, and Portland. N721US is seen against a backdrop of Waikiki, Honolulu.

This is an image of Northwest's Boeing 720B N728US (c/n 18421) in the fall of 1961 on Boeing's pre-delivery ramp in Seattle. Two other Northwest 720s are in this line-up, along with four destined for Eastern Air Lines.

Complementing Northwest's DC-8s were its Boeing 707-320Bs, the first of 41 707s they operated, which were delivered in 1963. This type was intended to replace not only the airline's DC-7s but also the handful of DC-8s.

The stylish Boeing 707-320 depicted in a new Northwest Orient color scheme, introduced a decade after the type first entered service. It could carry 140 passengers on trans-Pacific flights in a mixed-class configuration, or 165 passengers in an all-economy domestic configuration.

This is a pre-delivery picture of a Northwest Boeing 707-320B. Part of Northwest's specification to Boeing was for a "combi" configuration so that its 707 aircraft could be used for freight or for passengers or a combination of both. A 91-inch-by-134-inch forward cargo door was fitted.

When Northwest took delivery of the 707th Boeing 707 from Boeing on May 14, 1968, it was 14 years from the day that the 707 prototype was first rolled out. It was also an opportunity for a big publicity splurge. For the occasion, two pretty Boeing employees, Bonnie Carter (left) and Sandra Woodward, joined Northwest's Captain Paul Soderlind (NWA Director of Flight Standards), with Glen Doan (Second Officer Flight Engineer) on the right and pilot Dean Sunde on the left.

Passengers aboard Northwest Orient's Boeing 727s were given this card as a flight memento. The first three of the smaller 727-100 joined the Northwest fleet in November 1964.

Boeing 727s, mainly 727-200s, flew with Northwest until the retirement of the last one in 2003. This example, a 727-251 (N285US), was delivered new to Northwest in August 1977 and is pictured a decade later in Northwest Orient colors taxiing at Detroit.

Like the DC-9s, Boeing 727s were assimilated into the Northwest fleet from some of the airlines that were merged into Northwest. Still in partial Republic Airlines colors, Boeing 727-251 N721RW (c/n 21200), seen here at Detroit, was originally a Hughes AirWest aircraft (see Chapter Six.)

This image shows pre-delivery of Northwest Orient's first Boeing 747-151 N601US (c/n 19778) in May 1970. It is kept company with a Japan Air Lines and PanAm 747 on the Boeing ramp at Seattle. In mid-1966, Donald Nyrop announced Northwest's initial order for 15 of these huge 747 "jumbo jets" at a cost of $21 million apiece.

With the delivery of the first Boeing 747s, Northwest introduced a new Northwest Orient color scheme for its fleet. A new "compass" logo was adopted and the name "Northwest" was eliminated from the tail. The old faithful red tail was retained, though. N601US is pictured on a pre-delivery test flight over the Pacific seaboard of Washington state.

Able to accommodate 362 passengers in a mixed-seating configuration and cruise at 625 miles per hour, the massive Boeing 747s ordered by Northwest were powered by four Pratt & Whitney JT9D turbofan engines. Here Northwest officials accept delivery of their first 747 in May 1970.

Northwest Orient also consolidated its standing in Japan and throughout Asia with the establishment of an important hub operation at Tokyo. N613US, a 747-251B delivered in June 1971, is seen landing at an unequivocally Oriental destination.

With the word "Orient" now dominant in the airline's name, Northwest Orient consolidated its position as the U.S.'s main player in the trans-Pacific market. The first Northwest 747 schedule was flown on June 22, 1970 between the Twin Cities and New York. Five longer-range 747Bs and 747-200s joined the fleet in 1971.

With the flexibility of the 747-200, Northwest Orient was able to look to Europe as well as Asia in the quest for growth and new services. This 747-200 is seen nosed in at London Gatwick's south terminal "satellite." Northwest started services to Europe in 1979; the first Twin Cities to London 747 flight was on June 2, 1980, a service that Northwest has proudly continued on a daily basis ever since.

Boeing 747-251B N628US (note the Fleet No. 6628 on the nose-wheel undercarriage door) in Northwest Orient colors taxies for departure at Detroit in 1987. Beyond is a former Republic Convair 580 resplendant in the "new" Northwest colors. Also note the word "Republic" on the hangar beyond, partially erased but certainly not forgotten.

Pictured at Detroit in classic Northwest Orient colors, Boeing 747-251B N628US (c/n 22389) was delivered to Northwest on April 8, 1980, having flown for the first time at Seattle on March 21 of that year.

Like most major U.S. airlines, Northwest did not want to be left out in the competition for international flight supremacy. It had aspirations to join the ranks of airlines flying super-sonic transport (SST) jets as early as 1964. Several U.S. airliner manufacturers presented proposals in a competition administered by the FAA, including Boeing and McDonnell-Douglas. The Boeing 2707-200 was chosen to proceed to production in December 1966, although the whole program was cancelled by the U.S. Senate in March 1971. This image shows a model of McDonnell Douglas' proposal in Northwest colors with the small inscription "Orient Express" on the tail.

This Boeing model from 1979 was prepared when the Seattle manufacturer was courting Northwest Orient for orders for its new wide-body, medium- to long-range twin jet: the Boeing 767. The prototype 767 first flew on September 26, 1981, by which time Northwest had long since standardized on the Douglas DC-10.

Celebration of Northwest's 50th anniversary in 1976 was enhanced by the arrival of Daniel F. Neuman's Stinson Junior and Waco biplane (see end of Chapter One) at Minneapolis/St. Paul. One of Northwest's DC-10-40s, N155US, delivered new in December 1973, provides scale.

Shortly after the first long-range 747-200s were added to the fleet in 1971, an industry-changing order was placed by Donald Nyrop for fourteen DC-10s. The "shatter factor" was the choice of engine, Pratt & Whitney JT9Ds, for commonality with Northwest's Boeing 747s. General Electric CF6-50s were the engine of choice for most DC-10 customers. Northwest's were re-designated DC-10-40s, one of which is seen here at Orlando, Florida, in April 1984.

Northwest's fleet of DC-9s and derivatives was to grow to be the largest in the world, although they never actually bought a new "nine" themselves. This was mainly as a result of takeovers and mergers, principally of Republic. This ex-Eastern and Republic Douglas DC-9-14 (N8911E) was new in November 1966 and is seen at Detroit in 1987 in a hybrid Republic/Northwest scheme following the 1986 Northwest takeover of Republic. Northwest's last DC-9-10 series was retired by the airline in January 2005.

New in 1982, this McDonnell-Douglas MD-82 (N931MC) saw service with Republic and Texas-based Muse Air before the October 1986 Northwest merger with Republic. It wears a mish-mash of colors, retaining much of Northwest's 1970s and 1980s Northwest Orient color scheme, although when photographed at MSP in 1995 it also wore the tail design introduced in 1989 and the KLM/Northwest logo introduced following the 1993 anti-trust immunity alliance.

Northwest ordered an initial 20 Boeing 757-200s in 1983 with a follow-up order for another 10. The first delivery to Northwest Orient was of N501US in February 1985—the aircraft pictured, N504US, followed soon after and was named *City of Los Angeles*.

Northwest's 1980s order for Airbus A320s was complemented by interest in Airbus Industrie's long-range A330. This unusual, wingletted version (in the "old" Northwest Orient color scheme, but with the word "Orient" removed and "Northwest" substituted) is on a manufacturer's model that is now preserved and on display in the Northwest History Centre.

Convair 580s, originally with Michigan-based Simmons Airlines and acquired following the Northwest takeover of Republic and the Republic Express commuter operation, were withdrawn in 1987 and 1988. N7743U (s/n 390) spent just two years with Northwest; the last Convair was withdrawn from Northwest service on November 30, 1988 following nearly 30 years of service with North Central Airlines and successor companies.

Five

SOUTHERN AIRWAYS, WISCONSIN CENTRAL, AND NORTH CENTRAL

When North Central Airlines completed its takeover and merger with Southern Airways on July 1, 1979, it was the culmination of talks that had involved Southern for over a year. Other possible suitors included Allegheny Airlines, Ozark Air Lines, Piedmont Airlines, and Texas International.

Not only did North Central and Southern merge, but they adopted a new name, Republic Airlines, and as of October 1 that year, under the new Republic name, all flights adopted the new designator code "RC." The history and tradition of Southern brought to the new airline helped considerably in this geographical area of the U.S. air transport industry's difficult post-deregulation era (the Airline Deregulation Act became law in October 1978).

Southern was founded by Frank W. Hulse, a pilot, former manager of Augusta airport in Georgia, station manager for Delta Air Lines at Augusta, and then from June 1936 with colleague Ike Jones, the owner of Southern Airways, a local "fixed base operator" (FBO) and flight school. He expanded his FBO operations to Savannah and Atlanta, Georgia; Orangeburg, Anderson, and Greenville, South Carolina; and Birmingham and Muscle Shoals, Alabama. Hulse enlisted in the Army Air Corps in 1940 but was soon released, setting up flight training schools for the military throughout the south. On July 7, 1943, his organization became Southern Airways Inc. and on January 6, 1944, Southern Airways filed an application with the Civil Aeronautics Board (CAB) to start airline services in eight southern U.S. states.

A former Army Air Force C-47B (s/n 42-9316 and msn 13041) was Southern's first "large" aircraft, delivered to the Army in April 1944 and then to Southern on March 14, 1946 as N8820. It was leased to Piedmont Airlines. Other DC-3s (former C-47s and C-53s) were acquired, the second in June 1949 being N61450 (later N66SA, c/n 11631). It was this aircraft that inaugurated Southern's first scheduled passenger service on June 10, 1949, flying between Atlanta and Memphis with intermediate stops at Gadsden, Birmingham, Tuscaloosa, and Columbus. By the end of 1953, Southern was flying schedules to 29 cities over a route network totalling 1,914 miles. In November 1954, the airline boarded its 500,000th fare-paying passenger at Columbus. Expanding throughout the south, its DC-3 fleet grew, as services started to Panama City in Florida in June 1956. By 1959, the CAB had awarded Southern the rights to serve 17 cities, its fleet numbered 20 DC-3s and staff numbered more than 700.

Southern's history wasn't all smooth sailing; a pilots' strike took place in 1960, and the striking pilots established a rival airline: Superior Airlines. Southern suffered both union and political pressure, but always looking forward, Hulse ordered five former Eastern Air Lines Martin 4-0-4s to start replacement of his aging DC-3s. Southern's two-millionth passenger was boarded at Knoxville, Tennessee, on June 18, 1961, and on October 29 the first Martin 4-0-4 entered service. A total of 25 different 4-0-4s flew with Southern between 1961 and April 30, 1978.

Southern's last DC-3 service was on July 31, 1967, between Dothan, Alabama. and Memphis, Tennessee, overlapping with Southern's entry to the "jet-set" and its first Douglas DC-9-15 service (N91S) on June 15, 1967. 1967 was also the year of co-founder Ike Jones' death.

As further DC-9s joined the fleet—including stretched DC-9-31s—Southern's routes expanded as far north as Chicago. The early 1970s also brought tragedy to Southern: first on November 14, 1970, when a crash near Huntington, West Virginia, killed all on board; then on November 10, 1972, when DC-9 Flight #49 (N93S) captained by William R. Haa, from Chicago to Miami (via Memphis, Birmingham, Montgomery, and Orlando) was hijacked to Havana, Cuba. The hijacking lasted two days, and resulted in the 75 passengers flying to nine U.S. cities. They and the airliner all survived; the hijackers were arrested and their ransom money confiscated by the Cuban authorities. A further serious DC-9 crash occurred on April 4, 1977 near Atlanta with 81 passengers and four crew members on board. There were 23 survivors.

By 1974, Southern had a fleet of 24 DC-9s, including 13 DC-9-14s acquired from their Atlanta-based rival, Delta Air Lines. The Martin 4-0-4s soldiered on, flying low density short haul routes. In 1974, a $25 million investment commenced in a new Atlanta maintenance facility (now owned by Northwest) and Southern's first international service started on December 4, from Miami to Grand Cayman Island. The airline's flight attendants were also attracting passenger loyalty, their short "hot pants" and black pantyhose reminiscent of PSA's marketing ploys in California with mini-skirts. The noses of Southern's DC-9s were painted with a smiley face and the words "Have A Nice Day—Southern Airways."

Competition with Delta and Eastern Air Lines at Atlanta was inevitable (with 76 daily flights to 26 cities departing from Atlanta in 1975), but Southern also developed its Memphis hub and markets and by 1977 was flying 83 daily flights to 42 cities in 14 states. Consideration of the Boeing 737-300 was given by Hulse to expand capacity, but he opted to order four McDonnell Douglas MD-80s (DC-9-80) for initial delivery in 1980. 18-seat Swearingen SA226 Metroliner IIs (eight) were also ordered and entered service in June 1977 to replace the Martin 4-0-4s. They proved unpopular with passengers and difficult to operate at full capacity. The merger with North Central saw the demise of the Metroliners. By the time Southern was merged into North Central, it had 3,300 employees and was flying to 67 cities. By the time it became Republic Airlines, the statistics rocketed to 123 cities in 26 states, the District of Columbia, two Canadian provinces, and that single service to the Cayman Islands. Republic acquired Hughes Air West in California (see Chapter Six) less than two years later.

Like Southern and many other local service airlines in the U.S., Wisconsin Central Airlines (WCA) had roots World War II, although the airline wasn't incorporated until May 15, 1944. In 1940, the Four Wheel Drive Auto Company of Clintonville, Wisconsin, purchased two Waco biplanes. They were used as air taxis to fly the company's senior personnel back and forth between Green Bay (near Clintonville) and Chicago. A Howard DGA-15 five-seat, high-wing monoplane was then acquired and the route was flown daily.

Francis M. Higgins was elected WCA's first president and the two Wacos and single Howard were traded in against two twin-engine Cessna T-50 Bobcats. Despite a refusal from the Civil Aeronautics Board (CAB) in March 1946 against Wisconsin Central's application for provision of scheduled passenger air services in the region, WCA started intra-state services (which didn't require CAB approval) to six cities within Wisconsin on April 6, 1946. WCA's commitment that summer and fall caused the CAB examiner to rescind his earlier decision and on December 19, 1946, WCA were awarded a certificate giving them rights to fly services to 43 cities in the region. The important condition though was that the airline was to sever ties with Four Wheel Drive Auto Company!

Considerable re-organization and re-investment were required. Hal N. Carr was recruited from TWA, the Bobcats were replaced by three, nine-passenger ex-Trans-Canada Airlines Lockheed 10-A Electras and on February 24, 1948, WCA finally started regular scheduled services. The inaugural flight was between Minneapolis/St. Paul and Hibbing/Chisholm, Minnesota. A fourth Electra was soon added, and although most of the U.S.'s other regional airlines at the time were adding DC-3s to their fleets at anything up to $50,000 a piece, the Electras only cost $12,000 and served WCA's 11,400 passengers (carried in the first year) extremely well.

With two more Electras added to the WCA fleet, 32,630 passengers were carried in 1949 and WCA employed 228 people. As traffic on some routes grew, DC-3s finally arrived in October 1950; six were acquired from TWA at a cost of $450,000. The last WCA Electra service was flown on May 1, 1951, and that year 100,000 passengers were carried.

Despite continuing financial difficulties, and the resignation of Hal Carr, WCA were flying services from Chicago in the south, Brainerd in the west, Houghton in the north and Escanaba in the east. In 1952, Don Duff joined WCA as executive VP, further DC-3s were added to the fleet and services inaugurated to Fargo and Grand Forks, North Dakota but they were also given a stay of eviction from their headquarters at Madison. The airline decided to move its headquarters to Minneapolis/St. Paul and to change its name to North Central Airlines (NCA). A further merger between NCA and Lake Central Airlines was also proposed by the Purdue Research Foundation—this proposal dragged on into 1957, when it was rejected, and in the meantime NCA had almost disappeared due to bankruptcy. Hal Carr was appointed president at the age of 33 on April 15, 1954 and he quickly turned NCA around. By 1955, NCA carried 430,000 passengers per year, employed 900 people, and had coined the epithet "America's Leading Local Airline." By 1956, 24 DC-3s were flying some 100 flights per day with a route system stretching 3,240 miles and by the time of its 10th anniversary the following year, boarded 680,930 passengers and its two-millionth passenger overall in April 1957.

Turbo-prop Fairchild F-27s were considered, but economy caused an order for five Convair 340s instead, acquired from Continental and entering service in 1959 named "Super Northernliners." Further Convair liners were added, services were expanded in Minnesota, Nebraska, and the Dakotas, and by 1960 North Central carried over one million passengers in a year for the first time.

On April 26, 1965, the airline's last DC-3 was retired, eventually in 1975 being donated and preserved by the Henry Ford Motor Company museum at Dearborn, Michigan. 1965 also saw a $20 million order for North Central's first jets, five Douglas DC-9-30s, the first scheduled for 1967 delivery. Two million passengers were boarded in 1966, breaking its own regional airline record, five more DC-9s were ordered and a contract signed with Pacific Airmotive to convert 20 of its Convairs to Convair 580 status with Allison 501-D13 engines and other cockpit and interior up-grades. First of the Convair 580s entered service on April 1, 1967 and then on July 28, N951N, the first DC-9 arrived at Minneapolis/St. Paul—scheduled DC-9 services started on September 8.

North Central's 20th anniversary saw the airline with 2,600 employees and carrying over two million passengers a year. A serious crash of the airline's Convair 580s (N2045) at Chicago O'Hare on December 27, 1968 with the death of 27 of the 45 people on board was a tragedy but by October 1969 celebrations were again called for with the opening of the airline's new $15 million corporate headquarters and operations base at Minneapolis/St. Paul International airport. The same year three million passengers were carried but North Central posted its first loss in 16 years.

Another North Central Convair 580 crashed on June 29, 1972, involved in a mid-air collision with an Air Wisconsin Twin Otter, causing the loss of all on board. It was the same year that four more DC-9s were delivered and the year of another fatal accident involving a collision in thick fog on the ground between a North Central DC-9 and a Delta Air Lines Convair 880. Nonetheless, by the end 1973, the airline had boarded 4.5 million passengers and served 90 cities in 13 states and two Canadian provinces. By December 1975, Hal Carr handed over the reins to former president Bud Sweet and in 1976 the airline's fleet grew with the first 125-seat DC-9-50s arriving. By 1977, North Central's profits were up to $13.7 million; by 1978, profits were $22.1 million. Employees numbered 4,460, and the fleet numbered 59 aircraft, 36 DC-9s, and 23 Convair 580s.

In 1978, 13 new cities were added to their network, plus 17 "long haul" to assorted Florida destinations. Three 164-seat Boeing 727-200s were also ordered, but the fallout of the 1978 Airline Deregulation Act was forcing airlines to look at expansions and mergers as the business became even more fiercely cut-throat. Atlanta-based Southern Airways was cited, the two airlines jointly serving only eleven cities of the 67 it was serving, but without a single over-lapping route and a strong presence in the southern United States. Final approval for the merger by the Civil Aeronautics Board (CAB) was given in May 1979 and on July 1, 1979 operations by the new airline, now re-named Republic Airlines, were inaugurated. Republic then acquired Hughes Airwest on October 1, 1980, the combined Republic system now embracing 207 cities, more than any other airline in the U.S., with a fleet of 156 aircraft, 123 DC-9s, ten Boeing 727s and 23 Convair 580s and with orders for 21 more jets, five 727s, two DC-9-50s, and 14 DC-9-80s. The new Republic Airlines now employed 14,800, many based at Minneapolis/St. Paul. For traditionalists, the new Republic Airlines also continued to use the stylized flying mallard duck logo "Herman," which had first been adopted in the early 1950s by Wisconsin Central and then North Central Airlines.

Post-deregulation, most U.S. airlines were hemorrhaging cash and resources. Republic was no exception and by 1983 the company's combined losses were $220 million. In 1984, a new president and CEO, Stephen Wolf, was appointed. Wolf had arrived at American Airlines in 1966, was later with PanAm, and in 1982 became president and chief operating officer of Houston-based Continental Airlines. He stayed at Republic until 1986 and the Northwest takeover. In 1984, Republic reported a $29.9 million profit which increased to $177 the following year. Wolf was doing his job, but the airline was still burdened by debt. Government approval for the takeover of Republic Airlines by Northwest Orient, also based at Minneapolis/St. Paul, came on July 31, 1986.

Frank W. Hulse founded Southern Airways on July 7, 1943.

Southern operated from Atlanta, Georgia. One of its early Douglas DC-3s N63SA (c/n 7356) is pictured.

With a blue and yellow cheat line and white fuselage upper, Southern Airways' DC-3 fleet became one of the industry's smartest. The first DC-3 schedule was flown on June 10, 1949 linking Memphis (Tennessee) with Charlotte (North Carolina), Charleston (South Carolina), and Jacksonville (Florida) via Atlanta. This DC-3, N65SA, is pictured at Atlanta in 1961 in the last color scheme carried by DC-3s in Southern service.

By 1974, Southern had a fleet of 24 Douglas DC-9s which helped in the development of its Memphis hub. By 1977, Southern was flying 83 flights a day from Memphis to 42 different destinations. Some of the DC-9s ended up in Northwest's fleet—Memphis is now one of Northwest's three main hub airports.

Southern Airways' mini-skirted flight attendants helped catch the imagination of "Southerners"—a smiley face and "Have a Nice Day" were all part of the battle to attract customers in the intensely competitive market in Atlanta, where both Delta and Eastern were based.

Wisconsin Central Airlines' Howard DGA-15 was acquired in 1945 to fly daily service between Green Bay and Chicago.

Francis W. Higgins, Wisconsin Central's first president, sold the airline's two Waco biplanes and the Howard and purchased two wood and fabric Cessna T-50 Bobcats in the hope of starting scheduled passenger air services in 1946.

Three all-metal Lockheed 10-A Electra aircraft were acquired in 1948 for Wisconsin Central's first scheduled services. One of them is pictured sporting the airline's new "flying mallard duck" logo on the fuselage sides, a logo that was to survive in one form or another through to North Central and Republic, but was abandoned in the mid-1980s.

Wisconsin Central's first ex-Trans-Canada Airlines Lockheed 10A Electra was delivered to the Horlick Racine Airport in February 1948. Those who assembled include Hal Carr (Executive Vice President), Francis Higgins (President), and Gene Cleland (Superintendent of Communications).

73

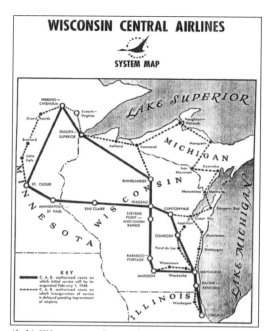

(left) Wisconsin Central Airlines' original route map dating from February 24, 1948, shows the initial 19 cities served by the airline. *(right)* This is the cover of an early Wisconsin Central timetable or "flight schedule" as it was called at the time. Already the mallard duck logo, nicknamed "Herman," was a prominent part of the airline's identity. "Herman" was the work of Milwaukee-based industrial designer Karl Brocken.

Wisconsin Central acquired six ex-TWA DC-3s, followed by many more before the airline's name change to North Central Airlines in 1952. One of these, in North Central colors, is seen in the 1950s in front of the airline's new headquarters at Minneapolis/St. Paul.

This is another North Central DC-3 with a slightly revised color scheme. Note the panoramic over-wing window and the airline fleet number in the white area behind the cockpit side window.

This cheerful group of individuals disembarks from North Central DC-3 flight number 784, overseen by the purser at the foot of the integral air-stairs. This is believed to be the inaugural flight on the new Detroit to Chicago route on May 1, 1955.

North Central Convair CV-340 N90858 (c/n 83) is pictured at Chicago (O'Hare) on March 25, 1961. This aircraft was originally delivered to Continental Air Lines in June 1953 and added to the North Central fleet in April 1959. It was later converted to a CV-580 and was destroyed in June 1972 in a mid-air collision with a Twin Otter near Appleton, Wisconsin.

This image shows North Central Convair CV-340 N90854 (c/n 49), another ex-Continental aircraft acquired in 1959 and also converted to a CV-580. The airline's colors at the time were predominantly white upper surfaces with yellow and orange trim lines. "Herman" and the "North Central" were very dark green.

Several U.S. airlines took advantage of the upgrade afforded by fitting Allison turbo-prop engines to their Convair 340/440s. They were re-designated CV-580s as a result. Note the large "paddle-blade" propellers on this North Central CV-580 at Chicago.

North Central was the last U.S. airline to decide to convert its Convairs to CV-580 turbo-prop status. Eventually their entire fleet of 35 was converted. N968N, at this point wearing the later, 1960s North Central "Apollo blue" colors, was an ex-Royal Canadian Air Force aircraft (designated a Canadair CL-66C) acquired by North Central in May 1967.

North Central's first DC-9-31 (N951N), pictured here, was delivered to Minneapolis/St. Paul on July 28, 1967, with services commencing on September 8 and bringing many cities on the North Central route network their first jet services. The color scheme is basically that of the Convairs, but with the airline's name stretched out along most of the fuselage length.

New stewardess uniforms were introduced in December 1969, featuring Apollo blue, a color in extensive use by the airline. Modeling these uniforms are (from the left) Judy Davies, Judy Ruff, Jill Kilgore, and Fran Seidler.

Pictured here are North Central stewardess class graduates in December 1970. They are, from left to right: (front row) Linda Wales, Romalee Rule, Doris Massman, Sandra Daugaard, and Loiuse Marvin; (back row) Trudy Cross, Judy Brawner, Karen Kuemmerlin, Lorraine Bell, Krecia Thompson, Karen Prins, Kathy Olslund, Linda Skedgell, Cecilia Byrne, Phillis Bonner, Suzanne Schroeder, Eva Woods, and Starr Skyberg.

This is another view of a North Central DC-9-30 while it bore the initial color scheme used on DC-9s. Also note the internal air-stair that slots into a small compartment below the front boarding door.

O'Hare was now every airline's first choice for services to Chicago, replacing Midway as Chicago's most-used airport. This eclectic mix in the mid-1970s shows a newly delivered North Central DC-9-30, along with a CV-580 and the rare sight of one of Delta's five Boeing 747s that they operated between 1970 and 1977. The DC-9 has a revised color scheme with the gold trim abandoned in favor of solid dark blues.

This early 1980s image shows a busy scene at Minneapolis/St. Paul. The DC-9-30 was one of two with which North Central experimented with a revised color scheme, with an American Airlines-style buffed metal finish. N961N (c/n 47405) is pictured.

Another picture taken at Minneapolis/St. Paul, this image shows the two alternative experimental color schemes displayed on passing DC-9s. Behind N961N (see previous image) is N963N in a "white top" color scheme. The tail of a company Convair CV-580 can just be seen.

This close-up shows N963N in the "white top" color scheme in an appropriately snowy setting.

A further variation on the North Central color scheme on one of 15 of the larger and "stretched" Douglas DC-9-51s that joined the North Central Fleet. It was delivered to North Central in June 1979 and immediately transferred to Republic, retaining the aqua blue-green color when Republic started operations on July 1, 1979.

Six

HUGHES AIR WEST AND ITS PREDECESSORS

Zimmerly Airlines was a small local service airline founded in 1938 at Lewiston, Idaho, by Bert Zimmerly. It was initially known as Zimmerly Air Transport. There were no associations between Zimmerly and Northwest, and there wouldn't be until mergers and takeovers caused an indirect union nearly 50 years later. Initially, Bert Zimmerly operated a small fleet of Cessna C-165 Airmasters on air taxi duties in Idaho. In 1944, he organized Zimmerly Airlines and acquired a fleet of three Boeing 247-Ds, one of the last airlines—other than in Alaska—to use this historic airliner in commercial service.

The airline's slogan "Wings Over Idaho" was initially seen on a single route that linked Lewiston with Boise, inaugurated on June 12, 1944, with a two-hour flight that cost a passenger $27 round-trip. By October 1945, the airline had expanded and was flying services from Pocatello to Coeur d'Alene via Burley, Twin Falls, Boise, and Lewiston. The morning flight departed Pocatello at 7:30 a.m. and after intermediate stops at the four other cities, its scheduled arrival time was 10:52 a.m. at Coeur d'Alene. The return over the same route departed at 11:30 a.m. and arrived back at Pocatello at 4:52 p.m.

In 1946, Zimmerly was merged and became Empire Air Lines based at Boise, Idaho. Empire flew their first service on September 28, 1946. Empire was one of the first U.S. airlines to be designated a "feeder airline" by the Civil Aeronautics Board (CAB). As airliners became more reliable and as remote small communities and cities began to demand their own air services, the nation's politicians and the CAB realized that a different level of airline was required that would rank below those of the expanding main-line carriers. On July 11, 1944, the CAB formally agreed to an airline in Texas (Essair) becoming the first official "feeder airline" in the U.S. In 1946, four more small airlines had joined the ranks of "feeder airlines," Empire Air Lines being one (West Coast Airlines of Seattle was another). Empire's first aircraft were the ex-Zimmerly Boeing 247-Ds, but anxious to increase capacity and status, the ubiquitous Douglas DC-3 soon joined the Empire fleet on March 10, 1948.

In March 1947, Empire's route structure was a "banana-shaped" line from Spokane, Washington, via Pendleton, Boise, and Burley, to Idaho Falls. The airline then expanded further from Idaho into additional destinations in Oregon and Washington. By November 1950, it had interline agreements with other airlines at Spokane for connections to Seattle and Vancouver; at Pendleton, Oregon, for connections to Portland; at Boise for connections to Reno and San Francisco; at Pocatello for connections to Salt Lake City; and at Idaho Falls for services to Great Falls and Lethbridge. Empire advertised their services as "Route of the Timesavers."

Advertising as an "air mail" and "air express" airline, Empire further encouraged air travellers to board their DC-3s with their slogan, "Relax . . . travel in deep cushioned comfort, arrive rested ready for work or pleasure. You are only a few minutes away from places formerly hours away."

Covering the hinterlands of coastal Washington and Oregon, it was perhaps natural that in 1952, Empire merged with West Coast Airlines, another DC-3 operator based at Boeing Field in Seattle—the date of the official merger was August 4, 1952. West Coast had been founded on February 1, 1950, and flew north-south coastal routes between Washington (Seattle) and

Oregon (Medford). Trading during 1953 as West Coast Empire Airlines, "Empire" was dropped and by November 1, 1954, the airline was simply West Coast Airlines with a comprehensive route structure covering the most populated areas in Idaho, Washington, and Oregon.

Throughout the 1950s, airlines were searching for the elusive DC-3 replacement, particularly in the territory that West Coast served, with short runways, density altitude problems, and high temperatures. West Coast was to pioneer such a replacement and was the world's first operator of the Dutch-designed 36/40 seat Fokker F-27 Friendship turbo-prop airliner, and began services with this type on September 27, 1958. This aircraft was the first of an initial West Coast order for four F-27s. The aircraft was in fact a license-built version of the Dutch F-27, built by the Fairchild Company of the U.S. following the signature of a licensing manufacture agreement in New York on April 26, 1956.

West Coast Airlines expanded, and while many other local service airlines in the U.S. were flying Convairs and Martins, West Coast had a definite edge. In the early 1960s, their "territory" had extended south to San Francisco and northwards to Calgary in Canada. Being ahead of the competition had always been West Coasts mantra and on September 26, 1966, it was one of the U.S.'s first "local service" airlines to put the DC-9-15 jet into service. It shared this honor with Bonanza, Ozark, Allegheny and Trans-Texas.

At the opposite end of the scale, West Coast also introduced their "MiniLiner" in April 1967—a "scaled-down fanjet" according to their advertising, but in reality it was a Piper PA-31 Navajo powered by two 310-horsepower Lycoming TIO-540 flat-six cylinder engines. This was yet another first for West Coast; its four-aircraft order was the first airline use of this type following the first production deliveries to executive aircraft customers in March 1967. The Navajos, although only able to seat seven (one passenger sat alongside the pilot during single-pilot operations) replaced West Coast's DC-3s on routes such as Sun Valley to Boise and between Sun Valley and Salt Lake City, Utah. The following year (on April 17, 1968) West Coast merged with Bonanza Air Lines and Pacific Air Lines to form Air West, but continued to use the Navajos to connect with Fairchild F-27 and DC-9 services.

Pacific Air Lines' history can be traced back to 1941 and the formation of Southwest Airways (which is completely unrelated to today's Boeing 737 operator, Southwest Airlines). However, the company was only certified as an airline on May 22, 1946, and flew its first scheduled service with DC-3s on December 2, 1946, linking cities along a route initially between Los Angeles and San Francisco (Santa Barbara to Paso Robles to Monterey/Carmel to San Jose) and later Medford, Oregon, specializing in one-minute stops at minor stations along the way. Southwest was able to achieve this claim with new passenger handling methods, the shorter turn-arounds giving greater operational efficiency, an objective that today's low-fare airlines came to quickly appreciate.

Southwest's DC-3s were fitted with internal air stairs to avoid the necessity of waiting for ground crews to wheel steps into place alongside the parked aircraft. Traveling pursers also sold tickets on board to save time and reduce costs at the cities at which they stopped. Southwest began operating non-pressurized Martin 2-0-2s in April 1953, aircraft that the airline purchased second-hand from Northwest Airlines.

Northwest had ordered 40 Martin 3-0-3s (later re-designated 2-0-2s) in June 1946 as part of its huge post-war expansion. Between 1948 and January 1951, six of the Martin 2-0-2s had crashed; the whole remaining fleet (21 aircraft) was removed from service by Northwest while investigations took place. Northwest then grounded its 2-0-2 fleet on March 17, 1951, many being leased to Transocean Air Lines and operated in basic Northwest colors. Four of these leased aircraft were then returned to Northwest and sold to Southwest, which operated them alongside their DC-3s. On March 6, 1958, Southwest Airways changed its name officially to Pacific Air Lines; Southwest had already unofficially called itself "the Pacific Air Line" for many years. Pacific operated 22 Martin 2-0-2s and 4-0-4s in all, including three ex-TWA 4-0-4s. Pacific received a Supplemental Type Certificate to increase passenger capacity of its 4-0-4s to 44 seats. The airline continued to operate its Martin 4-0-4s until April 9, 1968 and the official merger of Bonanza Air Lines and West Coast Airlines—PAC's last DC-3 was also retired, flying its last service on June 30, 1968. Pacific also flew 14 Fairchild F-27s between February 1959 and 1968. One of these, N2770R, crashed en route to Stockton, California, on May 7, 1964, when a passenger shot the flight crew and the aircraft crashed near San Ramon, killing all 44 persons on board. During the 1960s PAC suffered from severe competition, notably from PSA (Pacific Southwest Airlines) operating in the intra-California market with Lockheed Electras and then Boeing 727-100 jets. Pacific had acquired three Boeing 727-100s to match this competition and had ordered six Boeing 737s to replace the 727s.

This era of PACs Californian prop-liners is carried on in the present day by Jeff Whitesell of Oxnard, California, an ex-Delta Air Lines captain and president of Airlines of America. His aircraft, Martin 4-0-4 N40429 (s/n 14135), is now registered N636X, and although it flies nostalgia flights adorned in the 1950s Pacific Air Lines colors, it was originally delivered to TWA in 1952. Whitesell bought the aircraft in June 1994 in Pueblo, Colorado. After restoration, it flew again in early 1997 and has been an active memorial to this prop-liner and the operations of PAC ever since, visiting air shows around the country.

The other constituent of the U.S. West Coast group of airlines that were eventually merged into Republic, and then Northwest, was the local service Las Vegas-based Bonanza Air Lines. Originally a charter operator founded on December 31, 1945, the airline started intra-state services on August 15, 1946 using DC-3s. The airline was certificated on June 15, 1949 and flew its first scheduled service on December 19, 1949, flying between Reno, Las Vegas, and Phoenix. The airline was granted the rights on the Las Vegas to Phoenix sector from TWA.

Like many of the region's DC-3 operators at the time, Bonanza also ordered Fairchild F-27 turbo-props (in May 1956), receiving their first in February 1959. Bonanza flew 32 different F-27s in total; most were absorbed into the Air West fleet following the April 1968 takeover. Bonanza's growth was spearheaded in 1963 by its order for the Douglas DC-9, joining Delta and Air Canada with initial orders for the Long Beach-built jet. On March 1, 1966, Bonanza's first Douglas DC-9-11 jet entered service at Las Vegas. Bonanza had initially signed a letter of intent with the British Aircraft Corporation for their BAC-111 jet, but subsequently cancelled in favor of the DC-9.

Bonanza's aircraft had white fuselage upper surfaces with an orange cheat-line and orange tail, distinguished by the airlines characteristic "Big B" logo. Bonanza merged with West Coast and PAC on April 17, 1968. The "Big B" logo had several reincarnations after 1968—one of these was in the late 1970s at Las Vegas when DC-3 N101ZG was painted in a blue, green, and white scheme, but instead of the forward slope of the original "Big B," this had a reverse slope "B."

The most significant merger was of Bonanza, PAC, and West Coast under the name Air West, in April 1968. The fleets of these airlines as well as the geographical areas they served made a merger a logical business idea. Prior to this, in May 1964, West Coast's Nick Bez had unsuccessfully tried to acquire a controlling interest in PAC. Another proposed tri-partate merger was first broached in August 1967. Such mergers were still subject to the CAB's approval, but the advent of jet airliners, as much as anything, precipitated such mergers—and as the local service operators got together, it was the dawn of the growth of regional airlines within the U.S.

The CAB eventually approved the merger—the "OK" came from President Johnson himself—because international routes were involved (Canada and Mexico). Air West had a huge network of routes, totalling 8,800 miles. With the exception of the four Piper Navajos from West Coast, the new combined Air West fleet was wholly turbine-powered. Air West had Nick Bez as chairman, with former Bonanza chairman Edmund Converse as vice chairman and PAC president E. Robert Henry as the new president. The early fortunes of Air West weren't good—a complete failure of the airline's new computerized reservations system didn't help. Air West posted a first-year loss of $20 million.

With Howard Hughes still looking for involvement in an airline, after he'd given up his interests in TWA in 1960, it was a relief to Nick Bez, the majority shareholder in Air West, that he was able to conclude a sale to Hughes in the sum of $90 million. The Hughes Air Corporation took over Air West on July 21, 1969, with Hughes Tool Company owning 78% and Howard Hughes himself owning 22%. On April 1, 1970 the airline was officially named Hughes Air West. Irving Tague was installed as the airline's vice president of corporate services and general manager, but few of the former chief executives survived, although Converse and Henry were retained.

PSA was "wowing" its customers with late 1960s chic, mini-skirted flight attendants, bright colors, and blistering schedules. Hughes had to compete and in 1971 ordered a dramatic re-branding of Hughes Air West. Bright banana yellow was the adopted color. Aircraft, tickets, uniforms, vehicles, etc., were all subject to the corporate "yellowness." Los Angeles designer Mario Armond Zamparelli was commissioned to design the new yellow uniforms, which were visually stunning but uncomfortable to wear and keep clean, with their predominantly nylon and polyester fabric. Hughes Air West were headquartered in San Francisco with the fleet standardized to DC-9-10s, DC-9-30s, and the F-27s. The Navajos and Boeing 727s were retired.

Re-arrangements included the move to Seattle-Tacoma from Boeing Field in April 1971 and revised routings to increase average trip lengths. A mechanics strike between December 15, 1971 and April 1972 contributed to an annual loss of $3.3 million, but by 1972, Hughes Air West looked to increase its fleet and acquired 12 ex-Swissair and Continental DC-9-15s.

Routes were consolidated, and in the case of Mexican destinations, increased. Boeing 727-200s were ordered rather than the DC-9-50. Following Howard Hughes' death on April 5, 1976, there was little change; his Summa Corporation continued to control the airline. By that time, Hughes Air West was flying to 55 destinations, 48 of them with all jet service. The average sector lengths were also above 400 miles; management tried to increase sector lengths and fares still further. By the end 1977 the airline had a fleet of 49 aircraft.

Following deregulation, when CAB route awards ended, as did route subsidies (Hughes benefited from subsidies for service to 20 cities, totalling $9.7 million, in 1978), the competition became even more fierce. The airline was starting to expand eastwards with services from Phoenix linking Houston (Hobby), Milwaukee, and Des Moines. They were difficult times and in 1979 the airline posted a loss of $22 million, not helped by a two-month strike by ticketing and reservations staff.

In early 1980, the Summa Corporation announced that it had reached an agreement with Republic Airlines for the sale of Hughes Air West for $38.5 million. The airline changed hands on October 1, 1980, with Republic initially operating its new acquisition as a subsidiary, Republic West. It took until January 1983 for the last vestiges of Hughes Air West to be scrubbed from the new Republic Airlines.

Bert Zimmerly, founder of Idaho-based Zimmerly Air Transport and Zimmerly Airlines, is pictured with his first aircraft, a Cessna C-165 Airmaster.

Bert Zimmerly's ambitious local airline Zimmerly Airlines displays its three Boeing 247-Ds shortly before the creation of successor, Empire Airlines. This photo was taken in Lewiston, Idaho, in 1945.

This is the front cover of a c. 1945 Zimmerly Airlines timetable, with the by-line of "Wings over Idaho."

In March 1948, Empire Air Lines was able to dispense with its ex-Zimmerly Boeing 247s and commence operations with Douglas DC-3s. This unidentified lady was obviously having the time of her life. The caption on the back of the original photo reads "Queen for a Day."

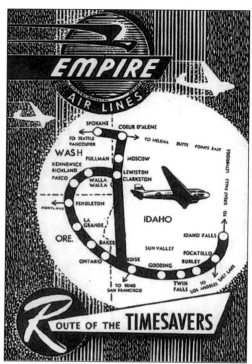

This is an extract from an early Empire Air Lines route map, the "Route of the Timesavers."

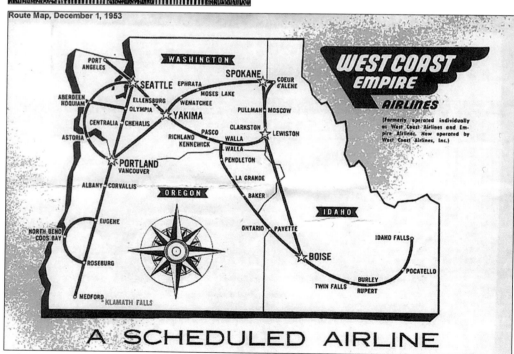

When Empire Air Lines and West Coast Airlines combined in August 1952, the new West Coast Empire Airlines had civil air transport in the states of Washington, Oregon, and Idaho pretty much stitched up. This is a route map from December 1953.

In the mid-1950s, like most other local service airlines of the time, the Douglas DC-3 was the aircraft of choice. N56589 is pictured here at Boeing Field in Seattle in the West Coast Airlines colors adopted after the word "Empire" was dropped from the name.

Pioneering the ubiquitous DC-3 replacement, West Coast Airlines ordered the Dutch-designed Fokker F-27 Friendship in April 1956 and was the world's first operator in September 1958. N2701 (c/n 3) pictured is the U.S.-built Fairchild F-27.

West Coast Fairchild F-27A N2701 (see previous photo) wears a new color scheme when photographed at San Francisco on December 26, 1965.

West Coast's pioneering choices of new equipment included the Douglas DC-9 and in September 1966 it became one of the first "local service" airlines in the U.S. to put the new jet into commercial service. N9104 was delivered on August 23, 1967, and later flew with Hughes Air West and Texas International, with whom it ended its days following a crash at Denver in November 1976.

The sister ship to N9104 (previous photo), West Coast's N9103 was delivered in December 1966, also moving to Hughes Air West and Texas International. The aircraft met its fate in a crash on March 17, 1980, at Baton Rouge, Louisiana.

This is a classic picture of a Southwest Airways Douglas DC-3 (N67589) taxiing to its stand at Oakland, California, in 1952 shortly before the airline introduced its first Martin 2-0-2s.

This West Coast Airlines advertisement coincided with its 1967 order for Piper PA-31 Navajos, or "MiniLiners," as the airline preferred to call them.

Gigantic new addition to West Coast Airlines. It carries seven passengers.

West Coast calls it a MiniLiner. It's the newest Piper. And a pip. It's also a major breakthrough in commercial aviation. No regular airline has ever before offered scheduled small-aircraft service. West Coast is the first. And there'll be a flock of these MiniLiners providing scheduled service between selected areas of the Northern West. Salt Lake City to glorious Sun Valley, for example. The MiniLiner: like a scaled-down fanjet. Quick, quiet, comfortable. And fun!

WEST COAST AIRLINES

This is a 1960 picture of a Pacific Air Lines Martin 4-0-4 N40436 (c/n 14171) following Southwest's change of name to Pacific in March 1958. Pacific operated its last scheduled 4-0-4 service in April 1967, when Fairchild F-27s took over many of the routes.

This photo taken by Chuck Stewart in San Francisco in July 1960 shows another of Pacific Air Lines Martin 4-0-4s. Pacific operated 22 different Martin 2-0-2s and 4-0-4s between 1952 and 1967, including three 2-0-2s leased from TWA in 1958–1959. Note the tails of two Pacific F-27s in the distance.

Fairchild F-27As were ordered by Pacific Air Lines in April 1958, with the first being delivered in 1959. N2774R (c/n 52) was delivered on June 11, 1959, later passing to Air West and Hughes Air West before being sold in Canada in September 1974.

Pacific Air Lines' F-27A N2776R wears a new color scheme in March 1967 in San Francisco. The airline operated 14 different F-27s, most of which were assimilated into the new Air West fleet following the merger of Bonanza and West Coast in April 1968.

Pacific operated its Fairchild F-27As alongside its Martin 4-0-4s, as this early 1960s picture at San Francisco shows, including another picture of N2774R (c/n 52). Some of the Californian "competition" in the shape of PSA (Pacific Southwest Airlines) and one of their Lockheed Electras can be seen.

Still flying the Californian skies in 2005 as a tribute to the heady days of Pacific Air Lines' Martinliners, this Martin 4-0-4 N40429 (c/n 14135), now registered N636X, was restored to airworthy condition and is flown and owned by Jeff Whitesell of Oxnard, California. It was photographed by Chuck Stewart over Oxnard in June 1997 and still flies enthusiasts and visits air shows to perpetuate the memory of what Californian commercial flying was like 50 years ago.

Bonanza Air Lines' Douglas DC-3 is pictured at San Diego, California, in the 1950s. Bonanza was based in Las Vegas and was another of the western U.S. "local service" airlines that grew rapidly in the 1950s and 1960s as air transport developed.

This picture of a Bonanza Air Lines' DC-3 N492 was taken at Oakland, California, in October 1960. The colors included white upper surfaces with an orange cheat-line and tail and the stylized "B" logo on the tail. Note the BOAC (British Overseas Airways Corp.) Boeing Stratocruiser tail behind.

Bonanza was not alone in its orders for Fairchild F-27A turbo-props, and with a total of 32 operated, constituted the largest fleet of the type before the merger to form Air West. Bonanza first ordered F-27As in May 1956. N146L (c/n 37) Fairchild F-27A, was known as the *Silver Dart* (it had Dart turbo-prop engines), is pictured here at San Diego, California. This aircraft was delivered to Bonanza in February 1959.

Mixing it with the "big boys," Bonanza Air Lines Douglas DC-9-14 N945L (c/n 45728) was delivered to the airline in December 1965 and entered service in March 1966. It is pictured here at LAX (Los Angeles International) which Bonanza served from its Las Vegas base.

With the Fairchild F-27As of Pacific, Bonanza, and West Coast, the newly formed Air West had the world's largest fleet (36) of the type in April 1968. This is an ex-Pacific Air Lines aircraft.

Illustrating the simple Air West colors, this Douglas DC-9-31 (N9335) was one of a batch ordered new by Air West and delivered in November 1969. It later joined the Republic Airlines fleet and is still part of the Northwest Airlines fleet.

"The Man," Howard Hughes, who longed to get involved in owning and operating an airline again after giving up his interests in TWA in 1960, acquired Air West in July 1969 and re-named it Hughes Air West the following year.

Two Fairchild F-27As are pictured: N1782, (ex-Ozark, Pacific Air Lines, and Air West), and N751L (ex-Bonanza and Air West). They wear the striking banana yellow color of Hughes Air West as part of the 1971 re-branding of the airline.

Yellow was the Hughes Air West color from 1971 onwards and flight attendants were very much a part of this yellow revolution, although the sole male representative in this photo seems a little fazed by his attractive companions!

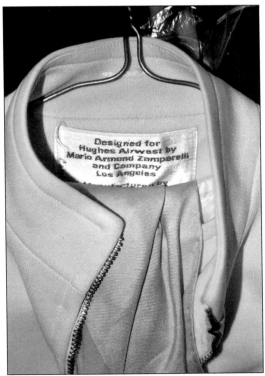

The 1971 yellow Hughes Air West uniforms are now museum pieces. Designed by Los Angeles designer Mario Armond Zamparelli, their nylon and polyester fabric was visually stunning, but extremely uncomfortable to wear.

Hughes Air West ordered Boeing 727-200s in a break from the airline's traditional use of DC-9s. N723RW was delivered in December 1976 shortly after Howard Hughes' death and was named *Spirit of Hughes Flying Boat*. Two of the other 727s delivered at this time were also given appropriate names: *Spirit of Gama* and *Spirit of the Racer*. This aircraft was transferred to Republic in 1980 and its contemporary sister ships were flying with Northwest until the type's final retirement in 2003.

This hybrid scheme, with the name "Republic" applied and a blue band deleting the "Hughes Airwest" titles below, was applied following the acquisition of Hughes Air West by Republic in 1980. DC-9-31 N9340 was delivered new to Air West in April 1969 and is seen here on approach to land at San Jose, California, in July 1981.

Although delivered to Eastern Air Lines in February 1968, Hughes Air West acquired this DC-9-31 (N921RW) in June 1978. It was assimilated into the Republic fleet in July 1979 and was flying with Northwest in March 1999 when pictured at Atlanta, Georgia. Behind is Atlanta's international concourse and downtown Atlanta—Northwest maintains an important DC-9 maintenance facility at Atlanta, part of the heritage of Southern's Atlanta base.

Seven

REPUBLIC AIRLINES

The 1978 Deregulation Act ushered in an era of freedom and competition to the U.S. airline industry, and Republic was a child of this post-deregulation era. Many new start-ups appeared and the era heralded many airline mergers. One of the biggest and first was the July 1, 1979 merger between Southern Airways and North Central Airlines, which became Republic Airlines, headquartered in the Twin Cities—probably because North Central was already based in Minnesota and was the bigger of the two merged airlines. The "RC" flight code of the new airline became universally adopted from October 1, 1979.

The geographical bonus of the North Central/Southern merger was that only 11 cities were duplicated on the two airlines' pre-merger route networks. Putting the two networks together created a route network that stretched through the whole eastern half of the U.S., from Florida and Grand Cayman in the south to Winnipeg, Canada, in the north and from New York to Denver. At its formation, Republic served 120 airports in 27 states. Expansion was also on the agenda and Republic soon launched new services from its pre-merger strongholds of Minneapolis/St. Paul, Detroit, Atlanta, and Memphis. The first service to the West Coast was launched from Minneapolis to San Diego via Las Vegas, using initially DC-9s until the first of an order for seven Boeing 727-200s, already ordered by North Central, started to arrive in February 1980.

Both airlines also had extensive commuter networks serving smaller towns and cities, Southern using its eight Swearingen SA226 Metroliners and North Central its 24 Convair 580s. The core of the two airlines' fleets were its Douglas DC-9s, 28 from Southern (DC-9-10s and -30s) and 48 from North Central (DC-9-30s and -50s), totalling 76 at the time of the merger. The Metroliners proved problematic and were sidelined as soon as possible. Services—particularly to some of Southern's former small destinations—were abandoned as they could not support DC-9 size aircraft.

The vigorous momentum of the post-deregulation U.S. airline industry meant that the directors of Republic couldn't rest on their laurels. They were soon scouring the U.S. for other merger candidates, particularly in regions of the U.S. they didn't yet serve, notably the West Coast. The former Air West, now Hughes Air West (see Chapter Six) was in their sights. The Civil Aeronautics Board (CAB) approved Republic's takeover of Hughes Air West on September 12, 1980, adding another 50 aircraft to Republic's fleet (42 DC-9s and eight Boeing 727-200s) and bringing the new Republic fleet total to 156 aircraft. Employees numbered 14,800. Republic Airlines West Inc. operated as a subsidiary to Republic until finally, in January 1983, all vestiges of the former Hughes Air West were buried for good. Republic added 42 new cities to its network; services within the states of Utah, Oregon, Washington, Idaho, and Montana, plus the Canadian province of Alberta, all became Republic territory for the first time.

Republic paid $38.5 million for Hughes Air West. Deregulation was generating unprecedented competition and yields were diminishing. Debt was also growing as interest rates rocketed and Republic's order for 14 new McDonnell Douglas MD-82s had to be financed. The whole philosophy of the airline's operations started to change as it developed from a mainly point-to-point operator to a hub and spoke operator. The hub cities of the pre-Southern/North Central era were developed by Republic, so Minneapolis/St. Paul, Detroit, Milwaukee, Memphis, Atlanta, and Phoenix were developed as the number of local service schedules to small cities decreased. By mid-1981, Republic had racked up a debt of $650 million and pay cuts were the order of the day. Sale of their 15 Boeing 727s was considered.

Bad publicity from two 1983 in-flight incidents (involving Republic DC-9 Super 80 and a DC-9-30), with bad fuel management procedures cited as the causes, gave the public no encouragement to fly with the airline—in some circles the word "Repulsive" replaced the airline's name!

On February 20, 1984, 42-year-old Stephen M. Wolf joined Republic as its executive vice president and was soon appointed president and CEO; he had formerly served as president of Continental Airlines. Republic bosses were already reducing the number of cities served, and by the end 1984 these were reduced to less than 100—Wolf also worked with the unions to squeeze additional concessions from employees and to increase efficiency.

Wolf commenced discussions on topics of "mutual interest" in 1985 with Steven G. Rothmeier, who had become Northwest Airlines' president on September 26, 1983, and CEO on January 1, 1985. Wolf introduced a major image change. Until this time, the Republic color scheme was still a throwback to the turquoise green and blues of North Central, accompanied by the flying mallard named "Herman." At Wolf's instigation, the new Republic colors were modernized to a white, light grey, and red scheme. The number of hubs was reduced to just Minneapolis/St. Paul, Detroit, and Memphis and the airline created Republic Express in June 1985 with BAe Jetstreams and Saab 340As to provide "passenger feed" to these hubs from the smaller cities, notably those around the Memphis hub. Many small airline operations were taken over under the Republic Express banner. In Detroit, Simmons Airlines was one of these.

For the mainline Republic operation, Wolf also ordered six Boeing 757-200s and supplemented the existing mainly DC-9 fleet with a further six second-hand DC-9s plus three Boeing 727s. Wolf continued to talk to Northwest, but airline pundits and executives were thrown many false scents, with Delta and American both being tipped as likely candidates for a takeover of Republic during 1985. Republic's stock had been at a depressingly low level of $3 in 1982, but with Wolf's charisma and business acumen, the price rose to $14. Wolf and Rothmeier continued their merger talks in strict security, with just Al Maxson and Ralph Strangis from Republic and James A. Abbott and John Edwardson from Northwest also in on the bargaining. By January 23, 1986, Rothmeier offered Wolf $17 a share, and almost immediately the boards of directors ratified this agreement. Northwest bought Republic in a cash-for-stock deal worth $884 million. Northwest was rocketed from the seventh-largest U.S. airline to the third- or fourth-largest, with 30,000 employees and 312 aircraft. The government finally approved the merger on July 31, 1986, and at the same time, Northwest started to drop the word "Orient" from all titles and promotional material.

This ex-North Central Convair CV-580 N3423, now with "Republic" boldly painted on the fuselage but still bearing "Herman" the duck on its tail, is pictured at Chicago's O'Hare Airport in November 1981.

Another "renegade" to join the Republic fleet was this ex-Southern Douglas DC-9-31, still in its Southern color scheme except for the name "Republic." N908H was originally delivered to Hawaiian Airlines in April 1970 before being sold to Southern in April 1976.

DC-9-31 N916RW is seen taxiing to the ramp, in full Republic colors, after landing at Las Vegas' McCarren Field in April 1982. This ex-Eastern Air Lines aircraft N8935E was new in January 1968, moved to Hughes Air West in July 1977 (when it was re-registered) and finally to Republic in July 1979.

This DC-9-31 delivered new to North Central in April 1968, and still wore that airline's colors when this photo was taken in Chicago in 1981. It also, however, bears the name "Republic."

With up to 137 Douglas DC-9s in its fleet, the majority of Republic airliner pictures feature DC-9s. On finals to land at Las Vegas, the former North Central DC-9-31 N967N is seen in Republic colors. The aircraft was converted to a DC-9-32 in October 1980.

Three brand-new Douglas DC-9-51s sit on the pre-delivery ramp at the Douglas facility at Long Beach, California, prior to delivery to Republic at Minneapolis/St. Paul in January and February 1980.

One of seven of the tri-jet Boeing 727-200s ordered originally by North Central arrived at Republic in February 1980. N720RC is seen here lining up for departure on the runway at Orlando International in Florida in 1984.

Stephen W. Wolf joined Republic from Continental Airlines on February 20, 1984, and was soon named president and chief operating officer. After leaving Republic following the 1986 merger with Northwest, he took up senior positions with Flying Tiger Line, the UAL Corp (United Airlines) and in 1996, U.S. Airways.

In October 1984, Wolf instigated a change of image for Republic, the old blue and turquoise green colors and "Herman" tail logo being replaced by a white with light gray and red horizontal trim as depicted on this DC-9-51 N780NC. A "traditional" Herman tail can be seen to the left.

This DC-9-51 N782NC, delivered new in January 1980, was the first to receive the new Republic colors and was rolled out from the paint hangar at Atlanta in October 1984. It is seen here at Miami in March 1987 having adopted the red tail and title of Northwest, but still wearing the basic post-1984 Republic colors.

101

Departing the Boeing plant in Seattle, N602RC was one of a batch of six Rolls Royce-powered Boeing 757-200s ordered by Wolf which featured the "new" Republic color scheme. Because of the engine inconsistency with the 757s delivered to Northwest, these Republic aircraft were sold to America West Airlines after the 1986 Northwest take over of Republic.

The first Republic Boeing 757-200 was delivered to the airline in December 1985, when it became the largest aircraft to fly with the airline. The type was used on heavily-trafficked routes to Florida and the western U.S.

Some of the relics of "Herman" and Republic Airlines have a corner of their own in the Northwest History Centre in Bloomington, Minnesota. This display cabinet features Republic clothing, timetables, logos, display models, and much more from the short-lived airline (1979–1986) which was a child of the 1978 Deregulation Act. When Southern and North Central merged to form Republic, they created the U.S.'s largest regional airline in terms of enplaned passenger numbers.

Eight

NORTHWEST AIRLINK, KLM, AND NORTHWEST CARGO

Steven Rothmeier became president of Northwest Airlines in September 1983. Northwest's domination of the U.S.-Orient market continued despite the dropping of "the Orient" from the airline's title during the mid-1980s. In 1984, Northwest Airlines started to operate as a wholly-owned subsidiary of NWA Inc. and the first moves of a massive fleet re-vamping were underway. In March 1985, the first two Boeing 757-200s arrived, heralding the start of disposals of Boeing 727s. The October 1986 acquisition of Republic Airlines also had a dramatic effect on its fleet (including a huge influx of additional DC-9s) and route structure, eliminating the home-town competition that Republic had generated at Minneaplois/St. Paul.

Despite this, in 1985, Minneapolis/St. Paul was served by 33 different airlines which in total handled 11 million passengers and generated 330,000 aircraft movements per year. At the time of deregulation in 1978, there were only nine airlines serving Minneapolis/St. Paul, handling an almost identical number of passengers but only generating 220,000 aircraft movements per year.

The 1984 signature of a marketing agreement with Grand Rapids, Minnesota-based Mesaba Airlines to operate as the first Northwest Airlink carrier serving its Minneapolis/St. Paul hub was significant. Mesaba, founded in February 1973, was operating services throughout Minnesota, South Dakota, Iowa, and Nebraska with a fleet of Beech 99 commuter aircraft. Following the Airlink agreement, Mesaba acquired Fokker F-27-200s to "feed" Northwest at its Twin Cities hub. Swearingen SA227AC's Metro IIIs replaced the Beech 99s and more F-27s were added. In 1992 the first of 25 De Havilland Canada DHC-8-102As (Dash 8s) were added to Mesaba's Northwest Airlink fleet. For a while in 1994, Mesaba was involved with Florida Boeing 737-200 operator Air Tran Airways (following acquisition of Austin, Texas-based Conquest Airlines), but this was spun off in 1995 coinciding with Northwest Airlines taking a 29.7% financial stake in Mesaba.

As the Airlink agreement consolidated, Minneapolis/St. Paul saw considerable expansion of services. Mesaba made a decision in March 1996 to commit to a fleet replacement with Saab 340s, all its F-27s, DHC-8s and Metro IIIs being retired as a result. By 1998, Mesaba had 1,800 employees and served 41 non-stop destinations in 17 U.S. states and Canada—all services provided non-stop from Northwest's Minneapolis/St. Paul hub. In October 1996, Northwest ordered 12 Avro RJ.85 jets for use by its Airlink partner and when these entered service in May 1997, they became known as Northwest Jet Airlink. By June 1998, Mesaba was flying to 91 cities in 19 U.S. states and Canada from both Minneapolis/St. Paul and Detroit using a mixed fleet of turbo-prop Saab 340s and jet RJ.85s. A total of 36 Avro RJ.85s were eventually delivered and the airline continues to operate under the Northwest Airlink banner from both of Northwest's northern hubs, now serving 100 destinations in 26 U.S. states and Canada.

The other major Northwest Airlink agreement was signed by Northwest in 1987 with Express Airlines 1. Founded in May 1985, and headquartered in Atlanta, Georgia, this airline's first codeshare agreement was with Republic Airlines, whose fleet of Convair 580s couldn't serve some of the smaller communities. Under the Express 1 name, initially as Phoenix Airline Services Inc., it operated as an Airlink carrier at both Minneapolis/St. Paul (starting December 15, 1985) and at Northwest's Memphis hub. On its first anniversary, Republic Express was operating 20 Jetstreams and seven Saab 340s in 32 markets. Northwest was happy to incorporate Express 1 into its Northwest Airlink codeshare network following the 1986 takeover of Republic. By the late 1990s, the Jetstream and Saab fleet had grown, and Northwest encouraged Express 1 to make a commitment to jet equipment. Express 1 was the launch customer for the Canadair Regional Jet (CRJ), part of a commitment for 42 aircraft, the first being delivered in April 2000.

In 1997, Express Airlines 1 became a fully-owned subsidiary of Northwest Airlines. It was re-named Pinnacle Airlines on May 8, 2002. Pinnacle has been publicly traded since November 24, 2004. The transition from turboprops to an all-jet fleet has now been accomplished, with the fleet exclusively comprising Bombardier CRJs, both the CRJ.200LR and the larger CRJ.440—a total of 139 CRJs are either in service or on order, operating services from all three of Northwest's main U.S. hubs, including an early 2005 order for an additional 10 CRJ.200s to be operated by Pinnacle. Pinnacle Airlines now employs a total of 3,000 people, including 925 flight crew, and operates 656 daily flights and under the presidency of CEO Phillip Trenary.

The late 1980s saw Northwest commit to orders for new aircraft and to a major image change. The new aircraft color scheme was quickly nicknamed "the bowling shoe livery." The first aircraft to appear with the new color scheme—red fuselage upper surfaces and grey fuselage sides transitioning to a white side and underbelly, topped by a new circular compass-like Northwest logo—were part of Northwest's 1986 order for the European-built Airbus A320-211s. The first Airbus was delivered to Northwest on June 8, 1989; the airline now has a fleet of over 150 A320 "family" aircraft, including over 70 of the smaller A319-100s. An order with Airbus for 16 of the larger, twin engine, long-range Airbus A330s followed, and at one stage, the prospect of Northwest ordering the four-engine sister ship Airbus A340 seemed likely. Both A330s (and A340s) were intended as replacement for Northwest's DC-10 fleet and some of its older Boeing 747-200 "Classics." The order for A340s never materialized.

In 1989, Northwest became privately held by a group of investors headed by Alfred Checchi, Gary Wilson, and Fred Malek, but in March 1994 the airline was returned to the public stock market. In January 1993, Northwest signed a pioneering agreement with the Dutch airline KLM/Royal Dutch Airlines following the granting of anti-trust immunity to the two airlines by the U.S. Department of Transportation. This agreement was also made possible following the 1989 privatization. Anti-trust immunity means that the two airlines can operate their transatlantic flights as a joint venture in relation to pricing, scheduling, product development, and marketing—it has also meant that Amsterdam (KLM's headquarters) effectively became a major Northwest hub. Initially the Northwest/KLM alliance resulted in a 15% growth in traffic per year, compared to an estimated 5% had the alliance not been formed. In August 1997, Northwest committed itself to a 13-year "enhanced alliance agreement" with KLM. Since this time most of the main-line aircraft in the fleets of both Northwest and KLM have carried an alliance logo, and to emphasize the agreement in 1999, a Northwest DC-10-30 (N237NW) was painted in a special dual Northwest/KLM design.

On January 26, 1998, Northwest announced another major, long-term alliance—one with Houston-based Continental Airlines, in which Northwest initially acquired a 14% equity stake. The alliance, which has continued into 2005, includes code-sharing, combined frequent-flyer schemes, co-operation between Continental and KLM, and in particular as there's little overlap between the route networks of the two airlines, greater flexibility and scope on ease of booking, ticketing, check-in, and luggage handling.

Another small slice of the Northwest "megalith" came to notice in March 1997 when the GHI-CA Corporation, a NWA Inc. subsidiary, acquired the Minneapolis/St. Paul-based airline Champion Air. Founded in 1987, Champion Air purchased the operator's certificate from MGM Grand Air in July 1995; Champion was operating vacation charter flights but had also specialized in charters to carry professional sports teams. Initially with a fleet of five Boeing 727-200s, now increased to 12 aircraft, Champion Air was effectively "bailed out" by Northwest and Carl Pohlad in March 1997. Northwest continues to own a 40% stake in Champion Air.

Northwest Cargo is now one of the world's major cargo airlines with a dedicated fleet of 12 Boeing 747 freighters (both 747-200 and 747-400 variants). It was founded in 1975 and took delivery of its first three Boeing 747-200F freighters in 1976. By 1996, Northwest Cargo was ranked fourth in the world in terms of air freight tonnage carried. There were many pundits who criticized the establishment of a dedicated freight carrier within Northwest, but the airline's knowledge and standing in the Southeast Asian market ever since 1946 was a trump card for the airline in establishing this element of their airline business.

In 1972, Northwest's cargo sales, including mail, totalled $32.4 million—by 1985, on Northwest Cargo's 10th anniversary, this sales figure had grown to $408.5 million and by 1997 was $790 million.

Northwest Cargo represented the airline's first presence in Europe, when in 1979 747-200F flights were first operated trans-Atlantic from Boston and New York to Glasgow (Scotland) and Copenhagen (Denmark).

Freight hubs are now operated by Northwest Cargo at Anchorage, Alaska, Tokyo, Japan, and Manila, the Philippines. Many other trans-Pacific Northwest Cargo schedules are operated, particularly from the U.S. west coast, to Bangkok, Osaka, Singapore, Beijing, Guangzhou, and Hong Kong. Northwest Cargo is now the No. 2 trans-Pacific cargo airline in terms of tonnage carried.

This Northwest booklet from March 1997 features the "50 Years Bridging the Pacific" logo at bottom right. The logo appeared on all of Northwest's aircraft during the 50th anniversary year of its first scheduled flight to Asia. As an aside, the leaflet proclaims that Northwest recycles enough paper products in one year to fill 27 Boeing 747s!

Often referred to as "the Red Sea," the "Gold Concourse" at Minneapolis/St. Paul is pictured during a traffic bank in June 1995 when the airline was using 50 gates. This mix of airliners includes Boeing 727s, an Airbus A320, DC-9s, and a DC-10.

Another busy scene at Minneapolis/St. Paul International depicts an afternoon traffic "bank" in June 1997, with downtown skyscrapers visible beyond.

Northwest's other main hub airport is Detroit. This picture taken in June 1997 shows a crowded international ramp dominated by Northwest, with a single British Airways interloper.

During the difficult times in the late 1980s and early 1990s, Northwest "re-trenched" to its three main hubs, in areas and markets it knew best. This image taken at Detroit is dominated by Northwest and Northwest Airlink aircraft.

The third major Northwest "hub" is at Memphis, Tennessee, pictured here in June 1995. This is the legacy of Republic Airlines, which chose Memphis as one of its three main hub airports in 1985. Northwest acquired Republic and continued to grow the operation, significantly through Northwest Airlink operator Express Airlines 1 (now Pinnacle), which operates nearly 50 percent of flights at Memphis.

One of Northwest's first Airbus A320s (N307US), pictured at San Francisco in 1990, was part of a ground-breaking order in 1986 which made the airline the U.S. launch customer for the European airliner.

N303US, an A320, is pictured pre-delivery over the coastline of the South of France in 1989. It was partly Northwest's commitment to a huge number of new aircraft in the late 1980s, falling passenger numbers, and declining revenue that resulted in the airline entering Chapter 11 bankruptcy protection in 1989. Restructuring was made possible by privatization in a $3.65 billion transaction.

As well as its A320s, Northwest also ordered other A320 "family" aircraft, which benefit from a commonality of flight decks, making crew interchanges easy and effective. The larger A321 joined the fleet, as did the smaller A319 N337NB (pictured).

Northwest's DC-9 fleet grew to become one of the world's largest, although the airline never ordered any new. In 1997, Northwest adopted a policy of refurbishment of its older aircraft, investing $125 million on life extensions for its DC-9 fleet. This ex-Austrian Airlines DC-9-32 (N987US), fitted with long-range fuel tanks, is pictured at the gate in Memphis in 1995.

Douglas DC-9-51 N766NC is an ex-North Central aircraft that was first delivered in March 1977, flying with Republic, and then, post-1986, Northwest. It is pictured here at Atlanta, Georgia.

In a time warp, on the occasion of Northwest's 60th anniversary in 1986, its European operation was publicized when this Air Atlantique Douglas DC-3 (G-AMPY) was painted in the airline's 1950s colors. At this stage, the name "Northwest" was painted on the fuselage, but by 1987 had reverted to Air Atlantique.

Northwest's commitment to Douglas airliners included its order for DC-10s. They were used extensively for trans-Pacific and trans-Atlantic service in the 1980s and 1990s. Two examples are seen here at London's Gatwick airport in May 1995, along with a company Boeing 747-200 to the left. Northwest's first trans-Atlantic scheduled passenger service was to Glasgow (Scotland) on April 28, 1980—service to London Gatwick commenced on June 2, flown initially with Boeing 747s. DC-10s were substituted later.

Douglas twin and tri-jets pass at Minneapolis/St. Paul in 1997. The DC-9-32 in the foreground (N611NA) and the DC-10-40 (N153US) both carried the Northwest/KLM circular logo (see next picture) following the 1993 alliance.

Since the January 1993 grant of anti-trust immunity by the U.S. Department of Transportation, the Northwest/KLM alliance has been the envy of the air transport world. This simple logo was subsequently displayed on the majority of aircraft flown by both airlines.

A special design was applied to Northwest's DC-10-30 N237NW (ex PP-VMW) in 1998 to symbolize the importance of the Northwest/KLM alliance. This aircraft, pictured at London's Gatwick airport, was purchased second-hand by Northwest in December 1997.

Boeing's tri-jet (the 727-100) first flew on February 9, 1963; the first was delivered to Northwest in November 1964. Subsequently, over 65 examples flew with the airline, mainly the larger 727-200s. One of these (N801EA) is pictured, part of a batch of nine acquired from Eastern Air Lines. Several of these were used by Northwest during the 1990s, under a service agreement with seven National Basketball Association teams and one National Hockey League team.

Boeing 757-251 N547US is seen at the gate at Minneapolis/St. Paul in 1997, with the arched roof of the main Lindbergh terminal beyond. The terminal was named after the famous aviator, Charles Lindbergh, who was born in Minnesota.

Boeing 747-251B N614US is pictured at London's Gatwick Airport. Twenty-two of this model of Boeing's famous "jumbo jets" were in the Northwest fleet, plus three of the earlier 747-100s, the first of which was delivered in March 1971.

Northwest was the launch customer for Boeing's new "stretched" 747, the 418-passenger capacity 747-400. The first of these aircraft, N661US, was delivered to Northwest in January 1989 as part of an initial order for 10 placed in October 1985. This card celebrates Northwest's "first" with the 747-400.

Northwest's "Worldplane," Boeing 747-400 N670US, featured special artwork depicting international scenes, and was introduced in 1997 to celebrate the 50th anniversary of the airline's first trans-Pacific flight.

The "Worldplane" featured different artwork on each fuselage side. This is, in fact, a huge model (about 40 feet long) that hung in the Mall of America in Bloomington, just to the south of Minneapolis/St. Paul International airport, dominating a kids' play area named "Camp Snoopy." This model now belongs to the NWA History Centre, which has had difficulty finding a suitable home for such a large artifact.

Pictured here is Simmons Airlines' SD.3-60 N370MQ, one of a fleet of 27 operated by the Marquette, Michigan-based commuter airline. Simmons also flew EMB-110 Bandeirantes and NAMC YS-11s. Simmons was founded in 1978 and became a Northwest Airlink affiliate serving the Detroit hub in 1987.

An ex-Simmons Airlines ATR-42-300, turbo-prop N425MQ, was delivered new to Simmons in 1987, shortly after the airline signed a franchise agreement with Northwest.

In an original Northwest Airlink color scheme, this Saab 340A (N329PX) was originally delivered to Express Airlines 1 and is pictured operating at Northwest's Minneapolis/St. Paul hub in June 1995.

A pair of Express Airlines 1 BAe Jetstreams in Northwest Airlink colors operate at Minneapolis/St. Paul in 1995. Express had a fleet of 25 of these British-built Jetstreams.

"Operated by Mesaba Aviation Inc." is the small inscription under the cockpit window of this Northwest Airlink F-27 Friendship 200. In the early days of the franchise agreement between Mesaba and Northwest, the large fleet of 15 F-27s were the mainstay of the airline's operation at Minneapolis/St. Paul.

Mesaba also flew a large fleet of Swearingen SA.227AC Metro IIIs alongside the F-27s, until the last was retired from service in 1997. Two are pictured here at Minneapolis/St. Paul.

Another type operated by Mesaba as part of theNorthwest Airlink franchise, represented in a fleet of 30, was the DeHavilland Canada DHC-8-102As. N852MA is seen here in May 1995. By 1999, the last DHC-8 had been retired, as large numbers of Saab 340s and the first Jet Airlink aircraft arrived in the Mesaba fleet.

Both Mesaba and Express Airlines 1 operated Swedish-built Saab 340s. N340PX, an Express Airlines 1 Northwest Airlink aircraft, is seen here at Minneapolis/St. Paul in 1995. The Northwest Airlink Saab 340 fleet grew to become one of the world's largest. To celebrate Mesaba's 25th anniversary in 1998, Saab 340B N439XJ was painted in a special color scheme.

Manual handling is a fact of airline life. This female operator loads packages onto a conveyor for shipment in a Mesaba/Northwest Airlink Saab 340 departing from Minneapolis/St. Paul in June 1995.

Two Mesaba Airlines Northwest Jet Airlink, British-built, Avro RJ.85s (derivatives of the BAe.146) are pictured on the ramp at Minneapolis/St. Paul in June 1998. The first RJ.85 (N501XJ) was delivered to Mesaba in June 1997. The four-engine jet was configured with 69 seats.

With the advent of regional jets other than the RJ.85, Northwest Jet Airlink ordered the Canadian-built Bombardier/Canadair CRJ. This type has become the sole type used by Pinnacle Airlines (former Express Airlines 1), with a current total of 129 of the models CRJ200 and CRJ440 (40-seaters) either in service or on order. This CRJ200 is pictured at Charlotte, North Carolina, the only evidence of its operation by Pinnacle and not Northwest being a small logo alongside the main entry door.

The logo of Memphis-based Pinnacle Airlines, Inc., which was re-named as such in 2002, is simple but effective. Pinnacle operates wholly as a Northwest Jet Airlink airline, serving the airline's three main hubs.

Open wide! One of Northwest Cargo's dedicated Boeing 747-200F freighters is seen here. These aircraft have a cargo capacity of 235,215 pounds, or 105 tons. The first 747-200F was delivered to Northwest in 1975. The Northwest Cargo fleet had grown in 30 years, from its first three Boeing 747-200Fs to a fleet of 12 by 2005. A joint U.S./Japanese aviation agreement, signed in 1998, helped Northwest Cargo "grow," including its resultant "fifth freedom" rights to carry passengers and cargo between any city in Japan and any city in the Asia/Pacific region.

This image of Northwest 747-200F, pictured in the late 1970s Northwest Orient era, demonstrates its capacity. Cargo can be loaded via the nose or via the special port side cargo door. Not obvious is the belly cargo capacity for smaller items, an attribute of most of its "passenger" aircraft.

Nine

NORTHWEST IN THE 21ST CENTURY

The big six U.S.-based airlines, including Northwest, are now commonly known as "legacy carriers." The 21st century has seen the fortunes of these carriers climb, then plummet. The aftermath of the 9/11 atrocities is commonly explained as the watershed for the shift from profitability and expansion to loss and re-examination. The number of airline passengers certainly dropped dramatically after 9/11. In addition, the travelling public has switched allegiance from full-service legacy carriers, such as Northwest, to what are referred to as low-fare carriers. Notable as well are the business travellers, who traditionally travelled with airlines such as Northwest in business-class accommodations at a premium cost, and who are now, due to economic constraints in all areas of business, flying coach class or flying on low-fare start-up airlines.

The legacy carriers have had to re-invent themselves, improve efficiency, and re-negotiate labor contracts with many of their employees' unions—Northwest Airlines is no exception in this respect. "Cost saving" and "improved efficiency" are the two phrases that crop up over and over again as the airlines' quarterly profit-and-loss figures continue to show a bleak outlook, compared to the heady days of profitability and growth in the 1990s. Yield is also critical, as ticket prices remain low—forced largely by low-fare competition—and the price of fuel escalates alarmingly. Late in 2004, Northwest completed the restructuring of a $975 million revolving credit line, a condition for the implementation of a $265 million concession package with its pilots which would involve an average of 15 percent pay cuts. Northwest also recalled 200 furloughed pilots in the first half of 2005 to cover a forecasted increase in flying activity.

In addition to its hubs, Northwest's traditional strength has been its international services, notably trans-Pacific to Asia, with 200 non-stop flights flown each week between the U.S. and Asia, more than any other U.S. airline. Northwest's new Airbus A330-200s are spearheading 21st-century expansion into the Asia/Pacific region, as DC-10-30s are retired and will be joined in 2008 by new Boeing 787-8s. On June 10, 2004, a new Portland, Oregon, to Tokyo daily direct service commenced, a route abandoned by United and Delta. The A330s are configured with 243 seats, 32 of them business class. From its Tokyo hub, Northwest is now serving 12 cities in the Asia/Pacific region. Feed into Portland from 28 cities, including those from code share partners Alaska, Horizon, Delta, and Continental, will also boost traffic on this new route.

At the end of 2004, Northwest announced a system-wide annual load factor of 80.2% (2.9% above the 2003 figure), as well as a traffic increase of 7.1% and capacity increase of 3.1% over 2003.

Although the Northwest/KLM alliance of 1993 was unprecedented and groundbreaking, the June 2004 announcement that Northwest (along with Continental and KLM) was to apply to join the SkyTeam Alliance headed up by Delta Air Lines and Air France, is likely to be of more significance long term. The application was ratified and Northwest (plus KLM and Continental) formally joined the alliance on September 13, 2004. Other existing members of SkyTeam are Aeromexico, Alitalia, CSA Czech Airlines, and Korean Air. The alliance already operated more than 14,000 daily flights, prior to the additions of Northwest, Continental, and KLM. SkyTeam was founded in 2000.

On October 1, 2004, Northwest announced that Doug Steenland was taking over as chief executive officer of Northwest Airlines, following Richard H. Anderson's decision to resign and move to the United Health Group. Steenland joined Northwest in 1991 as vice president; prior to this appointment, he was a senior partner at the Washington D.C. law firm Verner, Liipfert, Bernhard and Hand. Unfortunately, the financial outlook of U.S. legacy carriers such as Northwest showed little sign of improving. On January 19, 2005, the airline reported a net loss of $420 million for the last quarter of 2004, or $359 million, excluding unusual items. A full year net loss of $878 million resulted, compared to a 2003 net loss of $565 million.

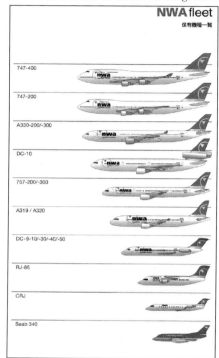

In early 2005, Northwest Airlines claims to be the world's fourth largest airline with its main strength in its hubs at Detroit, Minneapolis/St. Paul, Memphis, Tokyo, and Amsterdam. Employing 40,000 worldwide and operating a fleet of more than 400 airliners, Northwest accounts for 1,500 daily departures system-wide, including those of its Northwest Airlink operators Mesaba and Pinnacle. Northwest and its travel partners now serve more than 900 cities in more than 160 countries on six continents.

(*right*) Northwest's early 21st century fleet ranges from the Boeing 747-400 to the 32-seat Saab 340, and includes aircraft from Boeing, Airbus Industrie, Douglas, Bombardier, and BAe/Avro.

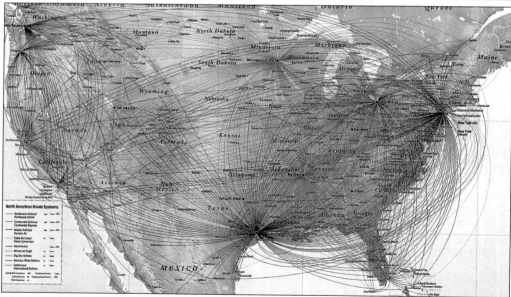

This 2004 North American route map illustrates the concentration of services from Northwest's main hub cities: Minneapolis/St. Paul, Detroit, and Memphis. Northwest's alliance with Continental Airlines shows areas of dominance centered on New York (Newark), Houston, and Cleveland, along with the Alaskan/Horizon alliance at SeaTac (Seattle/Tacoma) and Portland.

Many of Northwest's fleet were "parked" at Minneapolis/St. Paul following the aftermath of the 9/11 terrorist attacks—predominantly DC-9s and Boeing 727s. The optimism of the hangar-end mural was sidelined, as all airlines, including Northwest, set about recovering.

During 2003, a new corporate image was introduced, as displayed on this Airbus A320 pictured at Atlanta.

Another 2003 landmark was the opening of the new mile-long terminal at Detroit, dominated by Northwest Airlines and its newly delivered, long-haul Airbus A330 fleet.

This is an internal view of the new mile-long terminal at Detroit (Wayne County), or DTW. On the top right is the track for the electric mono-rail train that carries passengers rapidly to their departure gates.

In March 1997, the GHI-CA Corporation, a NWA Inc. subsidiary, acquired the Minneapolis-based Champion Air, a five-aircraft charter airline. MLT Vacations, another NWA Inc. subsidiary, uses Champion for vacation charter flights using their fleet of 12 Boeing 727-200s.

Another 21st-century Northwest innovation is e-check-in. Here, in the Lindbergh Terminal at Minneapolis/St. Paul, passengers check themselves in and choose seat assignments beneath a replica of Lindbergh's famous trans-Atlantic Ryan NYP *Spirit of St. Louis*.

Sporting the airline's new colors, Boeing 757-251 N538US taxies to its stand at Minneapolis/ St. Paul. Northwest has a fleet of 52 Boeing 757-200s, plus 16 of the larger capacity 757-300s.

All aircraft in Northwest's fleet are being painted in the new colors, including older DC-9s such as this DC-9-41 N755NW.

Northwest's fleet of Airbus A330s comprise two models, the 330-300 and 330-200. The first revenue flight by the latter (longer-range) model was on July 29, 2004, between Seattle and Tokyo (Narita). This was followed by the inauguration of the A330-200 on the Portland to Tokyo service on September 1 and the San Francisco to Tokyo service on October 1. Northwest will have seven of the A330-200s in service by the end of 2005. Northwest's Airbus A330 fleet are quickly relegating the DC-10 on international services.

127

Northwest had a fleet of eight Airbus A330-300s in service at the end of 2004. Options for 16 of the type were originally placed with Airbus in the early 1990s, the order only being confirmed in the next decade. This A330-300 is seen at the South terminal "satellite" at London's Gatwick airport in November 2004. While Northwest's A330 order was confirmed, they surprised airline pundits in May 2005 with their order for 18 (plus purchase rights for an additional 50) of the new Boeing 787-8s. Northwest's first 787 will be delivered in August 2008, the first 787s in North American service.

Northwest Airlines' important history is being preserved by the NWA History Centre. This October 2004 gathering at the Centre in Bloomington, Minnesota, includes Pete Patzke (with stick), Don Nyrop, and Al Carrivera. Steve Rothmeier also attended. It's the people who make an airline great.